CALL YOURSELF
A GUNNERS FAN?

THE ULTIMATE
ARSENAL
QUIZ BOOK

DEDICATION

This book is dedicated to Martin Cole, Dave Fletcher, Mike Lief, Stuart Tibber and Laurie Watson, who all stood on the North Bank back in the day; and special thanks are due to Stuart for his support of this project.

RACING POST

CALL YOURSELF A GUNNERS FAN?

THE ULTIMATE
ARSENAL
QUIZ BOOK

MART MATTHEWS

First published by Pitch Publishing on behalf of Racing Post, 2021

Pitch Publishing
A2 Yeoman Gate
Yeoman Way
Worthing
Sussex
BN13 3QZ

www.pitchpublishing.co.uk
info@pitchpublishing.co.uk
www.racingpost.com/shop

A CIP catalogue record is available for this book
from the British Library.

ISBN 9781839500787

Typesetting and origination by Pitch Publishing

Printed and bound in India by Replika Press Pvt. Ltd.

CONTENTS

INTRODUCTION

Hello Arsenal fans everywhere and welcome to what I hope is the most comprehensive quiz on your club in existence. I expect my inclusions and omissions will produce some argument, particularly where my choice of 'Highbury Heroes' is concerned, but that's all to the good.

A few words about the League Cup are necessary here. That was its original title when it appeared in the 1960/61 season. Among its many sponsors are five companies involving drinks. There's an early question. Who are they? To me it has always been the League Cup and always will be whatever transient sponsor it has at any particular time. It is a tedious task to be constantly looking up who was sponsoring it for every question I ask about it, and a fairly futile act into the bargain. Therefore, in this book it is the 'League Cup', end of story. Also, you will find no mention of super cups, club world championships, club world cups, inter-continental cups and their like. To me they are pointless excesses that have no meaning, are usually arranged a few thousand miles from where the supporters of the clubs involved live and leave a carbon footprint much larger than their value in players' and supporters' lives. They fill me with as much joy as international friendlies!

QUIZ No. 1

ANYTHING GOES

1. In the eight decades between 1930 and 2010, which was the only one that Arsenal did not win the league in?

2. Putting aside North London hostilities for the morning, Terry Venables acted as best man at the wedding of which Arsenal player?

3. In 1939 the Arsenal players and manager were asked to be involved in a 'who dunnit?' that was being filmed in and around Highbury. What was the film called?

4. Who is the only player to have scored a goal in a World Cup Final while at the club?

5. From 2012 onwards, AFTV has captivated and infuriated Arsenal fans and has built an impressively large following, not exclusively among Arsenal supporters, but also with those of other clubs who like to eavesdrop as Arsenal fans tear each other apart! Who owns and presents this YouTube channel?

6. What links these Arsenal players from different eras: Bob John, Alex James, Mel Charles, Charlie George and Thierry Henry?

7. Which Villareal player who shares his surname with a legendary motor-racing driver scored against Arsenal in a 1-1 draw in the Champions League quarter-final first leg in 2009?

8. In the 2002 World Cup Final between Brazil and Germany, a Spurs player and an Arsenal player opposed each other on the pitch for less than ten minutes. Who were the two players?

9. It sounds as though he couldn't move around enough to play football, let alone score a goal, but he did just that against Arsenal when they lost 2-0 to Borussia Dortmund in the group stage of the Champions League on 16 September 2014. Who was he and, for a bonus point, who scored their other goal?

10. What did Frank Moss, Arsenal's goalkeeper, do in a 2-0 away win at Everton on 16 March 1935 that is unique in the history of the club?

QUIZ No. 2

ARSENAL IN THE FOOTBALL LEAGUE – 1893-1915

1. As Woolwich Arsenal they made their entry into league football on 2 September 1893, in a 2-2 home draw with another club also making their league debut. Who were they?

2. 7-0 was a score Arsenal enjoyed a few times in those first seasons of league football. One club, situated geographically between Birmingham and Liverpool, were twice clobbered by that score by Arsenal in 1894/95 and the following season. Who were they?

3. It is extremely rare for a club's record win and record defeat to be against the same club, but that was Arsenal's experience. On 12 December 1896 they lost 8-0 and then, on 12 March 1900, they beat their conquerors 12-0. Who were they?

4. After eight years ensconced in mid-table, a couple of near misses eventually led to promotion to the First Division in 1903/04. Which Lancastrian club were they runners-up to?

5. A good start is always useful if you have your sights set on promotion, and Arsenal certainly made one. How many straight wins did they start that season with?

6. In Arsenal's period in the top flight, 1904–13, only one player was top league goalscorer for the club in more than one season. Who was he?

7. Arsenal were involved in a unique situation in English football in 1907/08. Their league record was as follows: played 38, won 12, drew 12, lost 14; goals for 51, goals against 63, points 36. Another club shared this record. Who were they?

8. Strangely, in that 1907/08 season, Arsenal played on both New Year's Eve and New Year's Day. It was not the finest 24 hours in the club's history, to say the least. They shipped 11 goals in the two

games against teams beginning with the same letter, six in Yorkshire and five the next day in the North East. Which two clubs inflicted the damage?

9. A player who entered the record books in 1905 when he became the first £1,000 transfer was Arsenal's top league goalscorer with 17 in 1911/12. Who was he?

10. 1912/13 is regarded as the worst season in the club's history. Relegation was accompanied by unwanted records. How many of their 38 league games did they win?

QUIZ No. 3

ARSENAL IN THE FA CUP - 1889-1915

1. Despite not getting started until 1930, Arsenal have now won the FA Cup more times than any other club. They took no prisoners the very first time they played in the competition, winning 11-0 on 5 October 1889. The club they beat shares its name with the surname of the actor who played Rodney in *Only Fools and Horses*. Who were they?

2. Until Chelsea beat Arsenal on their way to the 1915 final, only one London club had knocked Arsenal out of the FA Cup in this period. In fact, they did it twice, in 1896/97 and 1908/09. Who were they?

3. Arsenal reached their first two FA Cup semi-finals in successive seasons in 1905/06 and 1906/07. Which two clubs beat them?

4. Arsenal were involved in a frustrating epic at the first hurdle in 1899/1900 when they drew with New Brompton four times before losing to them in Gravesend after visits to Cold Blow Lane and White Hart Lane for replays. Who did New Brompton become in 1913?

5. Arsenal improved on the 11 goals they scored in 1889 when they won their first game in the competition in 1893/94. There's one of these in Middlesex and another in Kent. Who did they beat 12-0?

6. Arsenal knocked out a club from West London in 1902/03, and another from the same area the following season. Which two clubs were involved?

7. Despite some big FA Cup wins, it was hard work when you came up against northern clubs with a bit of pedigree in the competition. Two such clubs, Sunderland and Derby County, gave Woolwich Arsenal a reality check on their own ground, firstly in 1891/92 and again in 1898/99, both by the same unflattering score. What was it?

8. On the way to the semi-final of 1906/07, Arsenal beat two clubs from the same city. Which one?

9. The last club that Arsenal beat in an FA Cup tie before World War One was from South Wales and left the league in 1930. They share their initials with the guitarist whose spell with the Rolling Stones came between that of Brian Jones and Ronnie Wood. Who were they?

10. Here is a list of eight clubs Arsenal met in the FA Cup in these years. One of them I invented. Can you spot it? Crusaders, Kingston Pavilion, Swifts, Highland Light Infantry, Croydon Common, Sheppey United, City Ramblers and Second Scots Guards.

QUIZ No. 4

ARSENAL IN THE
FOOTBALL LEAGUE – 1919-39

1. Just before war arrived, two things changed. From 1913/14 they dropped 'Woolwich' from their name because they had upped sticks to north of the river, playing their first game at Highbury on the first day of the 1913/14 season. They were known as 'The Arsenal' in those last two pre-war seasons. When the war started Arsenal were in Division Two, but, magically, at its end they were in Division One. This cunning plan did not originate with Baldrick. Whose subterfuge was widely considered to have got Arsenal promotion without a ball being kicked?

2. Here's a crazy question! In that first post-war season of 1919/20 Arsenal finished mid-table, justifying to some extent their dubious elevation. Among their goalscorers were two occupations, a compass point, a contemporary physicist, a colour, a town from the North East and someone who shared his surname with a future Arsenal manager and player. How many of the seven can you get?

3. Arsenal have never, from this time on, lost their top-flight status, but it was a close-run thing in 1921/22 when they avoided the drop by winning their final two games against a Yorkshire club whose defeats sent them down instead. Who were they?

4. Arsenal were often a mediocre side in the 1920s, and it was hard to envisage the glories that awaited them in the 1930s. The last match of season 1927/28 saw them involved in a piece of football history when they drew 3-3 with the new champions Everton at Goodison Park. What was that piece of history?

5. Arsenal took their first league title in 1930/31, after FA Cup success for the first time the previous year. They scored 127 goals, with their third most prolific scorer Cliff Bastin getting 28. I don't imagine that has happened before or since. If you write the

full name of the leading scorer with 38 goals to his name you automatically write the surname of their second highest scorer on 31. Who were the two men?

6. Going from nought to nine, what was the only number of goals in a game that Arsenal failed to register in that 1930/31 season?

7. After finishing runners-up in 1931/32, Arsenal enjoyed three golden years which saw them equal Huddersfield's three titles in a row set in the 1920s. They recorded a nine and two eights and won 7-1 away on bonfire night at which Midlands club?

8. Their 1933/34 title came with 43 fewer goals to their name, so they wisely went out and bought Ted Drake to beef up the attack. He wasn't found wanting in 1934/35 when the title was won again, scoring at more than a goal a game. How many hat-tricks or four-timers did he get that season?

9. Cliff Bastin's 28 goals, as we've seen, couldn't even get him second place in 1930/31, but he was top scorer in both 1932/33 and 1933/34, the latter being his lowest total since 1929/30. How many goals did he win it with in 1933/34?

10. As the 1930s drew to a close, Arsenal won the league again in 1937/38, the fifth time in the decade they had done so. This side were clearly not as good as the earlier title winners. How many of the 42 league games did they lose?

QUIZ No. 5

ARSENAL IN THE FA CUP – 1919-39

1. When West Ham United knocked Arsenal out of the FA Cup in 1924/25 after two draws, on which London ground was the third match played?

2. Two other London clubs knocked Arsenal out of the FA Cup over this 20-year period, the first in 1920/21, with Arsenal gaining quick revenge the following season. The second club beat Arsenal in the FA Cup in both 1930/31 and 1938/39. Who were the two clubs?

3. Which Lancastrian club also knocked Arsenal out of the FA Cup twice in this period, in 1921/22 and 1937/38, both times on their way to the final?

4. In 1927/28 Arsenal went out in the FA Cup semi-final after facing West Brom, Everton, Aston Villa, Stoke and Blackburn Rovers. What else links these five clubs?

5. Which Welsh club knocked Arsenal out of the FA Cup on two occasions in the 1920s?

6. Arsenal met five clubs in FA Cup semi-finals during this time. Three of them are coastal clubs, of which two are found in the North East and one in the South. Who are the three clubs?

7. Which London club took a 7-0 hammering from Arsenal at Highbury in the FA Cup fourth round on 27 January 1934?

8. Arsenal recorded their biggest FA Cup win in this period on 9 January 1932 in the third round at Highbury when they won 11-1. Which Lancastrian club that had dropped out of the league at the turn of the century were on the receiving end that day?

9. Who scored four of Arsenal's 11 goals?

10. Arsenal scored an incredible 17 goals in three FA Cup ties in 1936/37, but it did them little good as they exited the competition in the sixth round via West Bromwich Albion. They had beaten Chesterfield 5-1, Manchester United 5-0 and Burnley 7-1. In that last game, which Arsenal player got four of the seven?

QUIZ No. 6

ARSENAL IN THE FOOTBALL LEAGUE – 1946-59

1. Arsenal were given a thorough working over by 6-1 on the first day of the first league season back after the war by a very hungry pack of animals who easily dodged their guns! Who were they?

2. That 1946/47 season was a triumph for one Arsenal forward who scored in the first six games and went on to net 29 goals in the 28 matches he appeared in. Who was he?

3. Arsenal were champions again in 1947/48 and put the cherry on the cake with an 8-0 home win over the bottom club on the season's final day, leaving them with an unpleasant memory to take to Division Two. They've never played top-flight football since. Who were they?

4. Less consistency the next season saw them in fifth spot in the league, but they could be brilliant on occasion. In three successive home games between 15 January and 26 February, against Sheffield United, Sunderland and Bolton Wanderers, they achieved something quite rare. What was it?

5. On 10 April 1950 Arsenal won 6-0 at Highbury, and then exactly one month later beat the same club 5-2 away on the last day of the season. Their opponents, who just avoided the drop, play in red and white stripes. Who were they?

6. Arsenal went to Old Trafford on the last day of the 1951/52 season needing to win by an eight-goal margin to deny Manchester United the league trophy and return to Highbury with it themselves. In the event, they lost 6-1, sadly allowing which club to sneak into second spot on goal average?

7. Champions again in 1952/53, Arsenal clinched the title with a 3-2 win at Highbury on the night before the famous 'Matthews' final. Arsenal's win over Burnley that night denied another Lancashire club the title. Which club?

8. On 2 March 1953 Arsenal won 4-1 at Sheffield Wednesday, with all four goals coming from a bustling centre-forward who got 19 that season. Who was he?

9. On 17 December 1955 Arsenal were leading Blackpool 4-0 with seconds remaining. At that point Arsenal's left-back Dennis Evans did something very rare indeed. What was it?

10. Arsenal managed third place in 1958/59 and early on in the season won successive games 6-1 away to Everton and at home to Bolton Wanderers. Which young centre-forward got four of the six at Goodison Park?

QUIZ No. 7

ARSENAL IN THE FA CUP – 1945-59

1. Cup football returned a year earlier than the league variety, and on 5 January 1946 Arsenal clearly weren't ready for it. Although they won the second leg 1-0, the game was already up after a 6-0 first-leg defeat at the hands of which London club?

2. Besides Highbury, which ground did Arsenal play five FA Cup ties on between 1947 and 1952?

3. What was unusual about Arsenal's FA Cup run in the 1949/50 season that culminated with their third win in the competition?

4. Which player, with a total of 13 goals, was their leading goalscorer in the tournament between 1945 and 1959?

5. Who were the only club Arsenal were drawn against three times during this period? In fact, with replays considered, they met seven times between 1947 and 1952.

6. Two clubs whose names begin with an 'N' lost and won FA Cup ties against Arsenal during the time in question. Who were they?

7. On their way to Wembley in 1950 and 1952, Arsenal were involved in semi-final replays, thus producing four semi-final matches in those years. Which Arsenal player scored in all four of those ties?

8. During this period Arsenal's programme was widely praised as one of the best on the market. For those supporters outside Highbury queuing up for their programme before the FA Cup sixth-round tie with Birmingham City on 3 March 1956, what shock was in store for them apart from the 3-1 defeat?

9. During this time Arsenal knocked a Lancastrian team out of the FA Cup on two occasions and did the same to a Midlands club that share their colours. Who were the two teams?

10. Arsenal knocked out a London club from the third flight of English football on 23 February 1952 by 3-0 at Highbury in the fifth round. Who did they beat?

QUIZ No. 8

ARSENAL IN THE FOOTBALL LEAGUE – THE 1960S

1. In 1960/61 Arsenal set a record for the club concerning successive draws. How many?

2. The new decade brought some signs of defensive instability, with 85 goals conceded in 1960/61. Which club that had three titles to their name in the 1950s, beat Arsenal 5-1 and 5-3 in the league that season?

3. Bonfire night of 1960 brought bad news. Arsenal didn't have far to travel home from this London ground but they were in no mood for fireworks after having just had a large one lit under them to the tune of six goals without reply. Who were their inhospitable hosts?

4. Boxing Day 1963 was the greatest-ever post-war day for goals in the top flight with 66 scored. What was Arsenal's contribution?

5. The vagaries of the fixture list meant that inside seven days in March 1964 Arsenal played against teams from the same city three times. Which city?

6. During the course of this same 1963/64 season, two Arsenal players whose names begin with the same letter scored hat-tricks, one against Ipswich Town and the other against Sheffield Wednesday. Who were the two players?

7. In 1967/68 you could have got a good price at one point about Arsenal finishing in the top half of the table, but they got there with a run of wins at the end of the season. How many?

8. In that same 1967/68 season an Arsenal player scored a hat-trick against Fulham and then, in 1968/69, got another against Sheffield Wednesday on his way to being crowned Arsenal's top league goalscorer of that year with 15 to his name. Who was he?

9. On 5 May 1966 Arsenal's game against Leeds United was accompanied by the lowest attendance post-war at Highbury. To the nearest 500, what was it?

10. As the decade died there was no real sign that this team could 'do the double' in the near future. Although fourth place was achieved in 1968/69, two poor runs in 1969/70 left them in 12th place. The worst of those two runs started in December and comprised how many games without a league win?

QUIZ No. 9

ARSENAL IN CUP COMPETITIONS – THE 1960s

1. The 1960s were not happy years for Arsenal where the FA Cup was concerned, and the successes in the decade of another club we won't mention in that competition were an added irritant. Which club knocked them out in successive years in 1962/63 and 1963/64, both times at Highbury?

2. In 1966/67 and 1967/68 it happened again when which Midlands club ousted them from the FA Cup two years running?

3. In the FA Cup of 1962/63 Arsenal played in three cup ties. Who was the only player, a Scottish winger, to score for them in all three matches?

4. Which Midlands club did Arsenal beat in a replay after a 3-3 draw in 1963/64 but then get knocked out by in the FA Cup of season 1968/69?

5. Which Arsenal forward scored a hat-trick in an FA Cup fourth-round replay against Bolton Wanderers on 22 February 1967?

6. What round of the FA Cup was the furthest one that Arsenal reached in the decade?

7. Arsenal were one of a number of clubs that turned their noses up at the new competition known as the League Cup. They gave it a wide berth for six years, but finally gave it a go in September 1966, when they were drawn at home to a club from the third tier of English football. They made hard work of it, drawing 1-1 and then by the same score in the replay, necessitating a third game which Arsenal won 5-0. Which club made life awkward for them?

8. Which Arsenal forward scored in all three of those games before decamping across London to Chelsea?

9.   When Arsenal beat Scunthorpe United 6-1 in the League Cup on
     25 September 1968, which player, who also left to join another
     London club in Spurs, scored Arsenal's only League Cup hat-trick of
     the decade?

10. Who, in the 1967/68 season, were Arsenal's first-ever opponents
     in a League Cup semi-final? If you need a clue you can find their
     ground of that time in the name of the club that beat Arsenal in that
     year's final.

QUIZ No. 10

ARSENAL IN THE FOOTBALL LEAGUE – THE 1970s

1. Did anyone see that coming? Arsenal achieved something that even the 1930s team failed to do. They won the League and the FA Cup in the same season in 1970/71. Three Highbury favourites played in all 42 league matches for the club. Who were they?

2. Arsenal's worst performance of that season came in September when they lost 5-0 away. Unfortunately, it was on *Match of the Day*, and there weren't many judges tipping them to win the league after that. Who beat them?

3. Which two Arsenal players scored hat-tricks during that season's league programme?

4. How many games did Arsenal win in succession from 2 March until a draw with West Brom on 24 April?

5. Which Scottish player, dubbed 'the new George Best' before he was ready for such nonsense, scored his first goal for Arsenal on 10 January 1970 in a 2-1 defeat at Old Trafford against Manchester United?

6. 1973/74 saw Arsenal finish tenth with a unique club record from their 42 league games. What was it?

7. Arsenal slumped to 16th in 1974/75, missing relegation by four points, and then to 17th in the following season. In 1976/77 they fared much better in finishing eighth, much to do with a new centre-forward who scored four goals against the team he had joined Arsenal from, which must have pleased them no end! He got one in a 2-0 away win and a hat-trick in a 5-3 win at Highbury. Who was he?

8. In that same 1976/77 season, an Arsenal central defender played in 33 games and scored twice. The odd thing was that his two goals came in the same game, a 3-0 home win over Leicester City. Who was he?

9. Arsenal were getting better towards the end of the decade and in 1978/79, although they finished only seventh, they won a thrilling FA Cup Final. They registered five goals three times in the league that season, and supporters were no doubt pleased that all three games were against fellow London clubs, who went down 5-0, 5-1 and 5-2. Who were the three clubs?

10. Arsenal's most consistent performer over the decade never missed a game in three of those seasons and missed just one in two more. Who was he?

QUIZ No. 11

ARSENAL IN CUP COMPETITIONS – THE 1970s

1. A much better decade for Arsenal in the FA Cup began with two appearances in the final in 1971 and 1972, with contrasting fortunes. They beat the same club after a replay in both semi-finals of those years. Which club?

2. In the next season, 1972/73, Arsenal were the victim of the romance of the FA Cup when they lost to Sunderland in the semi-final. Who scored in four FA Cup ties in a row and ended up their leading goalscorer in the competition?

3. Which Midlands club did Arsenal knock out of the FA Cup in 1970/71, 1972/73 and 1974/75, but lose to the only time they met in the League Cup in 1974/75?

4. Arsenal were not such a good proposition in the League Cup in this decade. How many times did they fall at the first hurdle?

5. Which Arsenal player scored a hat-trick in a 3-1 away win in an FA Cup third-round replay against York City on 7 January 1975?

6. Which Arsenal player scored in every round of the FA Cup run to Wembley in 1977/78, but couldn't manage one in the final itself?

7. On their way to that FA Cup Final in 1978, Arsenal beat three clubs whose names begin with a 'W' in successive rounds. Who were they?

8. In that same season, Arsenal reached the League Cup semi-final where they lost over the two legs to Liverpool. On their way to that semi-final they had beaten two sides from the same city. Which city?

9. Similarly, in the 1978/79 season, this time in the FA Cup, on their way to winning it they put out two clubs from the same city in the fourth and fifth rounds. Which city was it this time?

10. Arsenal had to play 11 games to win the FA Cup in 1979 and no fewer than five in 17 days to get past which club in the third round?

QUIZ No. 12

ARSENAL IN THE FOOTBALL LEAGUE – THE 1980s

1. Arsenal finished third in 1980/81 when their only ever-present was a newly signed defender who was to become a regular in the side, making over 400 appearances before joining Newcastle United in 1988. Who was he?

2. Arsenal won the last game of that 1980/81 season by 2-0 at Highbury, but their visitors still had a smile on their faces. Who were they, and why were they smiling?

3. Which ex-Chelsea and QPR player scored twice when Arsenal won 5-0 at Leeds United on 8 November 1980?

4. Although Arsenal finished fifth in 1981/82, they scored just 48 goals. It was only five days short of which month before Arsenal managed three goals in a game?

5. On 29 October 1983 at Villa Park, which Arsenal player scored five times in their 6-2 win?

6. Arsenal finished seventh in both 1984/85 and 1985/86. Which right-back signed from Nottingham Forest made an impressive start to his Arsenal career, missing just six games in the three seasons from 1984/85?

7. Arsenal finished fourth in 1986/87 and George Graham and Don Howe improved the defence. However, the football was sometimes a hard watch. At one point in the season they scored just one in how many games?

8. 1987/88 brought sixth place in the league and a hat-trick for new centre-forward Alan Smith in a 6-0 win over which club on 29 August 1987?

9. 1988/89 brought the most dramatic finish to any season before or since when Arsenal snatched the title out of Liverpool's hands in the last seconds of their Anfield encounter. Which three men played in all 38 league games?

10. During that momentous season, Arsenal scored twice from the penalty spot in the league. Who got both of them?

QUIZ No. 13

ARSENAL IN CUP COMPETITIONS – THE 1980s

1. The early 1980s were tough to take for Arsenal fans, being knocked out of the League Cup in 1980/81 and the FA Cup in 1981/82 by the same club. Which club was it? Look away now!

2. As if that wasn't bad enough, after working their way to the semi-finals of both competitions in 1982/83 they were beaten in both of them by the same club. Which one?

3. As the Gunners went tumbling out of the League Cup in the fourth round on 29 November 1983, extremely ancient supporters of the club might have been reminded of a January day in 1933. Which club repeated their feat of half a century ago?

4. Which club from Lancashire did Arsenal knock out of the League Cup two years running, in 1985/86 and 1986/87?

5. Which club broke Arsenal hearts in the 1988 League Cup Final and also knocked them out of the FA Cup in 1985/86?

6. In the third round of 1985/86 Arsenal were given a fright at Grimsby before they finally prevailed 4-3. Whose hat-trick was a major contribution to their cause?

7. Arsenal knocked out just one London club from a lower division in either cup competition over the decade. It happened in the FA Cup third round on 9 January 1988 in a 2-0 win at Highbury. Who did they beat?

8. Which player, who moved to Ipswich in 1984 after playing 280 games for Arsenal in all competitions, scored in the League Cup for the club in each of the first four years of the 1980s?

9. Which club did Arsenal put out of the FA Cup in 1984/85 and the League Cup in the following season? The FA Cup game went to a replay and Arsenal scored seven goals for the only time in cup competitions in the decade, if that helps!

10. On 31 January 1987 Arsenal won an FA Cup tie at Highbury 6-1, and then went to the ground of the club they had beaten and won 6-1 again in the League Cup on 19 September 1989. Who were the club?

QUIZ No. 14

ARSENAL IN THE LEAGUE – THE 1990s

1. 1990/91 provided a great start to the new decade, bringing with it another title, this time with a comfortable seven-point margin. Which Midlands club were the sacrificial lambs on the last day of the season at a Highbury in celebratory mood, and which Arsenal player scored a hat-trick in a 6-1 win?

2. Arsenal had a superb defensive record in the 1990/91 season, losing just once in 38 outings. How many goals did they concede and who were the only club to beat them?

3. There were five London clubs in the First Division at the time besides Arsenal. They were Chelsea, Crystal Palace, QPR, Spurs and Wimbledon. Surprisingly, given the fact that they won the league, Arsenal did the 'double' over just one of the five. Which one?

4. What was odd about the month of October 1993 in Arsenal's 1993/94 season?

5. George Graham was dismissed during the 1994/95 campaign over 'bung' allegations concerning the transfer of John Jensen, the midfielder from Brondby. It became something of a running joke that he would never score for Arsenal. Eventually he found the net once in 137 games for the club, at Highbury on 31 December 1994. It didn't matter much as Arsenal lost 3-1, but to which club?

6. 1995/96 was the year of Bruce Rioch's management of the club, and Arsenal finished fifth with two expensive newcomers getting off the mark. David Platt scored at Everton in a 2-0 win, while Dennis Bergkamp scored twice in a 4-2 home win over Southampton. Which two Italian clubs sold them to Arsenal?

7. In 1996/97 which two ex-Arsenal players became caretaker managers of the club until cries of 'Arsene Who?' were heard?

8. It didn't take long before everyone knew who he was as he led Arsenal to the 'double'. After Blackburn Rovers had won 3-1 at Highbury on 13 December 1997, Arsenal had lost four of their last

six games and no one was talking titles. From that date on they went on an unbeaten run to the league title of how many games?

9. The next season was very frustrating because they came close to another 'double' before losing out to Manchester United on both fronts. In their penultimate game, on 11 May 1999, an unlikely 22-all draw would have given them the title! They lost 1-0 to which club who would have been happier if Arsenal had won it?

10. In April of that season Arsenal beat Wimbledon and Middlesbrough 5-1 and 6-1 in successive games. At Middlesbrough which Arsenal player scored with a clever backheel that has often been shown on TV?

QUIZ No. 15

ARSENAL IN CUP COMPETITIONS – THE 1990s

1. Arsenal won 5-0 at Huddersfield in the League Cup second-round first leg on 21 September 1993, making the second leg a rather superfluous affair. Which Arsenal player scored a hat-trick at Huddersfield?

2. When Arsenal became the first club to do the domestic cup double in 1993 they beat London clubs in the semi-finals of both the FA Cup and the League Cup. Which two teams lost out at that stage in the two tournaments?

3. Which Yorkshire club did Arsenal beat three times in four seasons in the League Cup in the 1990s?

4. Arsenal were drawn against this club at the first hurdle in the League Cup in both 1994/95 and 1995/96. The collective score over the four matches was 15-0 in Arsenal's favour. Which opponents would have been pleased to hear the referee's whistle at the end of the fourth game?

5. Which London club did Arsenal play three years running in domestic cup competitions in the 1990s? They met in the 1992/93 League Cup, the 1993/94 FA Cup and in that same tournament the following year.

6. Which Yorkshire club did Arsenal get drawn against three times during the decade, ending up, because of replays, playing them seven times in all?

7. Which London club knocked Arsenal out of the League Cup in both 1997/98 and 1998/99?

8. In the FA Cup fifth round of 1998/99 at Highbury, Arsenal beat the same side twice with a 2-1 scoreline on each occasion. The second match was required after a dispute about one of Arsenal's goals in the first game. Who were their opponents?

9. Which Arsenal player missed a vital penalty in the FA Cup semi-final against Manchester United in 1998/99?

10. A crazy question to end with! Can you, with the clue provided in each case, name the following six clubs that Arsenal have knocked out of either of the domestic cup competitions during the decade?
    a) Lady Godiva
    b) The 1851 Great Exhibition
    c) Alan Ayckbourn
    d) Glovemaking
    e) Michael Parkinson
    f) One half of the Boat Race

QUIZ No. 16

ARSENAL IN EUROPE - 1963-80

1. Arsenal's first experience of competitive European football came in the Inter-Cities Fairs Cup in 1963, and it didn't take long for them to make their mark, winning their first game 7-1 at Highbury against Staevnet. They were a combined side of clubs from which city?

2. The downside of that first year in Europe was the size of the crowd at Highbury for that first game. It proved to be the lowest of the season. To the nearest thousand, what was the attendance?

3. Arsenal went out to Liege in the second round that year, but when they next competed in the tournament in 1969/70 they ended up winning it! Along the way they had another 7-1 Highbury win when they beat Dinamo Bacau in the quarter-final. In the semi-final and the final itself they accounted for two clubs that began with the same letter. Who were they?

4. Arsenal defended that Inter-Cities Fairs Cup trophy in 1970/71, but went out in the quarter-final. They might have had other things on their mind that season! Which German club knocked them out on the away-goals rule?

5. Because they were league champions in 1970/71, they made their first entry into the European Cup in 1971/72, where they accounted for Stromgodset and Grasshoppers of Zurich before losing to the eventual winners of the competition in the quarter-final. It proved to be the only time in their six seasons of European football in this period where they lost both legs of a tie. Who beat them?

6. 1978/79 saw their first foray into the UEFA Cup where, after beating Lokomotiv Leipzig, they got past Hadjuk Split before going out to a side that reached the final where they were beaten by Borussia Moenchengladbach. Who were they?

7. Having won the FA Cup in 1979, Arsenal's sixth season in Europe saw them play in their fourth different competition. This time it was the European Cup Winners' Cup and they went heartbreakingly close to landing it, losing on penalties after a 0-0 draw against which club?

8. On 9 April 1980 they drew 1-1 at Highbury in the first leg of that European Cup Winners' Cup semi-final against an Italian side that weren't overly interested in playing football. It was a disgusting exhibition that was meant to soften up Arsenal for the second leg and most judges gave them little chance. Who were the club that was supposed to be playing football against Arsenal that night?

9. The second leg witnessed one of the great nights in Arsenal history when they stunned the Italian crowd with a 1-0 win to go through to the final. Who got the vital goal?

10. Who, with 11 goals, was Arsenal's leading scorer in the six seasons of European competition covered in this section?

QUIZ No. 17

ARSENAL IN EUROPE - THE 1990s

1. After reaching the European Cup Winners' Cup Final in 1980, the rest of that decade proved very disappointing in Europe. In fact, they met just three opponents in those ten years. However, in 1991/92 they were in the European Cup again, going out to Benfica at the second hurdle. Before that they had knocked out Austria Memphis, who sound like a strange mixture of Mozart and Elvis! In their 6-1 first-leg win at Highbury, who came up with four goals?

2. Back in the European Cup Winners' Cup in 1993/94, Arsenal ended up winning it. In the second round they beat Standard Liege 10-0 on aggregate, scoring seven times in the away leg. Who was the only Arsenal player to find the net in both games?

3. In a hard-fought semi-final against PSG in 1993/94, Arsenal drew 1-1 in Paris before whose goal put them in the final when they won the second leg 1-0 at Highbury?

4. Alan Smith's fine goal in the final in 1994 brought the trophy back to Highbury when they overcame which Italian Club?

5. Back in the same tournament the following year, they came within an ace of winning it again when they lost in the final to which Spanish club?

6. Which Arsenal player scored in all eight matches leading to that final?

7. Who scored Arsenal's goal in that final of 1994/95?

8. Arsenal got into the European Cup again in 1998/99, although it was now calling itself the Champions League when that was increasingly breaking the Trades Descriptions Act! Arsenal went out in the group stage. Where did they play their three home games in the competition that year?

9. Although the actual final was in the year 2000, Arsenal's 1999/2000 UEFA Cup run is best covered here. Which French club, that they had met in the previous year's Champions League, did they defeat over the two-leg UEFA Cup semi-final?

10. Which club beat Arsenal on penalties after a 0-0 draw in that UEFA Cup Final of 17 May 2000?

QUIZ No. 18

ARSENAL IN EUROPE – THE 2000s

1. In the three years from 2000/01 to 2002/03, Arsenal played 35 games in the Champions League without getting beyond the quarter-final. Who were the only club they met more than once in those three years, Arsenal's place in the competition ending after playing them on each occasion?

2. Who scored a hat-trick in a 3-1 away win over Roma in the Champions League on 27 November 2002?

3. Things looked bleak for Arsenal in the Champions League in 2003/04 when they took just one point from their first three group matches. A late Ashley Cole strike gave them victory over Dynamo Kiev in their next game, before they produced a stunning 5-1 away win and ended up winning the group. Which club did they beat 5-1?

4. Which club put paid to their hopes 3-2 on aggregate in the quarter-final that year?

5. In 2004/05 in the Champions League, Arsenal were undefeated in their six group games but went out to which German club at the first knockout stage?

6. In 2005/06 Arsenal reached the Champions League Final for the first time in their history. They played 12 matches to reach that final, coming up against the likes of Real Madrid and Juventus. Their defence was magnificent, as could be shown by reference to the 'goals against' column for those 12 games. What was that figure?

7. Whose header put Arsenal in front in that Champions League Final in 2005/06 against Barcelona?

8. In 2006/07 Arsenal went out in the first knockout round of that same tournament after a 1-1 draw at The Emirates in which Alex scored for both sides. He put through his own goal to give Arsenal the lead in the 58th minute before putting Arsenal out by scoring for

his club seven minutes from the end. Who were his club?

9. In 2007/08 Arsenal recorded a 7-1 win in the group stage before finally going out in the quarter-final. Who did they beat 7-1 and who knocked them out?

10. Losing the 2008/09 Champions League semi-final to Manchester United was a painful affair. Which Italian club had Arsenal beaten on penalties in the first knockout encounter that year?

QUIZ No. 19

ARSENAL IN EUROPE – THE 2010s

1. In the 2012/13 Champions League, in the round of the last 16, Arsenal were outplayed at home in the first leg when Bayern Munich took away a 3-1 advantage for the second leg. Arsenal turned in a great performance by winning the second leg 2-0 in Germany, but went out on the away-goals rule. Which two players scored for Arsenal?

2. Which Arsenal player got the first hat-trick of his career on 1 October 2014 in a 4-1 home Champions League win over Galatasaray?

3. Arsenal could be frustrating on occasion. On 4 November 2014, in the group stage, they led 3-0 at home half an hour from the end, but finished up drawing 3-3 with which club?

4. In 2014/15, Arsenal repeated the pattern of two years before when, in the round of the last 16, they lost 3-1 at home before winning 2-0 away and going out again on the increasingly absurd away-goals rule. Who beat them this time?

5. In 2016/17 Arsenal suffered the biggest aggregate defeat by an English club at the knockout stages of the Champions League when they were hammered by the same score home and away by Bayern Munich. What was that score?

6. Arsenal were not used to playing on Thursday nights, and it was doubly galling in 2017/18 to be in the Europa League when Spurs were sitting at the top table. However, Arsenal made the most of it and reached the semi-final where, after a 1-1 home draw with Atletico Madrid, they lost 1-0 in the second leg. The goalscorer was someone who had irritated Arsenal a few times already. Who was he?

7. In the round of 32 in 2017/18, Arsenal won 3-0 away at Ostersunds, where one of their goals was an own goal by a certain Mr Papaglannopoulos, and I thought that would be a great question

along the lines of who is the longest-named player to score for Arsenal, congratulating myself that it was a clever question because he wasn't actually an Arsenal player. However, the plan went up in smoke when, after a bit of counting, I found an Arsenal player with a longer name. Who was he?

8. Arsenal were in the Europa League again in 2018/19 and put in a great effort to reach the final under a manager with a pedigree in the competition. Up to half-time in the final against Chelsea everything was even, but an abject second-half performance cost them dearly. One of the Arsenal players was the only Englishman on the field. Who was he?

9. Once again UEFA demonstrated the idiocy they are renowned for in forcing Arsenal and Chelsea fans to spend four-figure sums and travel half way around the world to watch their clubs. Which country did UEFA choose to host the Europa League Final of 2018/19?

10. Which club knocked Arsenal out of Europe three times during the decade?

QUIZ No. 20

ARSENAL - SEASON 2000/01

1. In 2000/01 Arsenal finished second without unduly troubling Manchester United. The team was undoubtably weakened by the sale of two players to Barcelona pre-season. Who were they?

2. Only once in the season were eight goals scored in an Arsenal game and this came at Highbury in the third match of the season when they beat which London club 5-3?

3. New signing Robert Pires scored his first Arsenal goal in a 2-1 away win on 21 October 2000 against which London club?

4. In that 2000/01 season Arsenal were solid at home, losing just once in their 19 games at Highbury, that defeat coming on 14 April 2001 at the hands of which northern club?

5. During the season Arsenal won and lost a game 6-1. The two teams met each other in the 1963 FA Cup Final if that helps any! Who were they?

6. Which Arsenal player got a hat-trick in a 5-0 win over Newcastle United on 9 December 2000 at Highbury?

7. Which new Arsenal player got off the mark for them on 16 September 2000 in a 2-1 home win over Coventry City?

8. Arsenal had a great FA Cup run that ended in a frustrating final against Liverpool. In the fourth round another London club had provided them with two own goals when they knocked them out 6-0 at Highbury. Who were they?

9. Which two other London clubs would Arsenal have been very pleased about knocking out of the FA Cup?

10. Which club that Arsenal had met once in an FA Cup Final ended their League Cup progress at the first opportunity?

QUIZ No. 21

ARSENAL - SEASON 2001/02

1. A fabulous season that ended with the league and cup double and an undefeated away record. It doesn't come much better. In which month did Arsenal lose for the last time in the league?

2. There was even greater satisfaction in clinching the title at Old Trafford with a 1-0 win on 8 May 2002. Who scored the winner for the men in the gold shirts?

3. Who were the only team Arsenal failed to beat in the Premier League that season, losing 2-1 at home and drawing 1-1 away?

4. Arsenal conceded four goals just once in the league when they lost 4-2 at home to which London club on 4 November 2001?

5. Who was the only Arsenal player to score in five successive league games? They came against Charlton Athletic, Spurs, Ipswich Town, West Ham United and Bolton Wanderers, all in April 2002.

6. Whose penalty beat Spurs at Highbury on 6 April 2002?

7. Which Arsenal defender scored at home to Newcastle United in an FA Cup replay and away to the same club in the league?

8. The only domestic trophy Arsenal didn't win was the League Cup, where, after wins over Manchester United and Grimsby Town, they lost 4-0 in the quarter-final. The only consolation for Arsenal fans was that the team that knocked them out went on to beat Spurs in the final. Who were they?

9. Which Arsenal player, against Newcastle United at Highbury on 18 December 2001, managed to get sent off when the game was already over?

10. 11 May 2002 was a day of celebration at Highbury, with Everton providing the opposition and obligingly going down 4-3. Who got the winner against his old club?

QUIZ No. 22

ARSENAL - SEASON 2002/03

1. Arsenal finished second in the Premier League and won the FA Cup for the second year running. Since the war only two other clubs had won the FA Cup twice in a row. Who were they?

2. Who was the only Arsenal player to make over 50 appearances in all competitions for the club?

3. Only one club did the league double over Arsenal, winning 2-1 at Highbury in October and 2-0 on their own patch in March. Who were they?

4. Which Arsenal defender came off the bench 23 times in all competitions during the season?

5. Which French defender scored his first goal for Arsenal in a 2-1 home win over Everton on 23 March 2003?

6. When Arsenal beat Southampton 6-1 near the season's end an unusual thing happened. Their six goals came via two hat-tricks by players whose names began with the same letter. Who were they?

7. In the run to the FA Cup Final, Arsenal accounted for Oxford United in the third round before being drawn away to a Hampshire based non-league club in the fourth round. This club waived the right to home advantage and made some much-needed money by visiting Highbury, even if they did go down 5-1. Who were they?

8. Which club in the following round did Arsenal knock out of the FA Cup for the third successive year?

9. Who was Arsenal's top scorer in the FA Cup in 2002/03? He also scored in the only League Cup tie the Gunners played that season, when they lost 3-2 at home to Sunderland.

10. The Arsenal team that beat Southampton in the FA Cup Final that year contained three players whose surnames began with the same letter. Who were they?

QUIZ No. 23

ARSENAL - SEASON 2003/04

1. Although Arsenal have done the double three times in their history, many would claim that winning the Premier League unbeaten in 2003/04 was the club's greatest moment. They conceded just 26 goals in their 38 games. Did they let more in at home or away, or a 50-50 split?

2. Only two clubs avoided defeat in the league against Arsenal. Unsurprisingly, one of them was Manchester United. Who was the other?

3. Which club took three hidings from Arsenal during the season for an aggregate score of 13-2? They lost 5-0 and 4-1 in the league and 4-1 again in the FA Cup.

4. Who was the only Arsenal player not to miss a league game?

5. Who scored his first goal for Arsenal in a 2-1 win over Chelsea in the FA Cup fifth round?

6. Which club did Arsenal beat in the FA Cup but lose to in the League Cup?

7. Which French player was Arsenal's top scorer in the League Cup?

8. Two sendings off in one question! Firstly, what was significant about Franny Jeffers being sent off in the Community Shield? Secondly, which ex-Arsenal player was sent off against Arsenal following an incident with Ashley Cole at Highbury on 1 February 2004 while playing for Manchester City?

9. Thierry Henry did something that hadn't been seen at Highbury for over 50 years when he got back-to-back hat-tricks on 9 and 16 April 2004. Which two clubs suffered by 4-2 and 5-0?

10. On 9 May 2004 Arsenal beat Fulham 1-0 in the Premier League with a Reyes goal. Where was the match played?

QUIZ No. 24

ARSENAL - SEASON 2004/05

1. Who was the only player to be on the pitch at some stage in all of Arsenal's league games in 2004/05?

2. Despite relinquishing the league title, Arsenal won the FA Cup rather fortunately on penalties against Manchester United in 2004/05. Which United player missed from the spot?

3. On 22 August 2004 Arsenal equalled the previous number of top-flight games without defeat when they came from 3-1 down to win 5-3 at Highbury. Who did they beat and whose record did they draw level with?

4. Three days later, a 3-0 Highbury win gave them the record. Which club from Lancashire did they beat?

5. Which Italian player who Arsenal had purchased from Parma ended the season as their top scorer in the League Cup, with two goals to his name?

6. Which city's two clubs did Arsenal play in the League Cup that season?

7. Arsenal's unbeaten record in the league stood at 49 games when it came to an end on 24 October 2004 in a game that went out of control at the end after a controversial penalty sealed Arsenal's fate. Which club did they lose to, as if you didn't know, and by what name was the unsavoury, or possibly savoury, incident in the tunnel after the game known as?

8. In March and April of 2005 both Portsmouth and Norwich City were beaten by hat-tricks at Highbury from the same player. Who was he?

9. Arsenal began the season by beating this club 4-1 away, and then, at the end of the season, beat the same club 7-0 at Highbury on 11 May 2005. Who were they?

10. Two incidents on the south coast to end with. Which Arsenal player got the winner when Arsenal won 1-0 at Portsmouth on 19 December 2004, and which Arsenal player was sent off in a 1-1 draw at Southampton on 26 February 2005?

QUIZ No. 25

ARSENAL - SEASON 2005/06

1. Against which London club on 1 February 2006 at Highbury did Sol Campbell substitute himself after feeling responsible for two goals that Arsenal conceded?

2. Arsenal's biggest win of the 2005/06 season came on 14 January 2006 by 7-0 at Highbury in the Premier League. Who did they beat, and which midfielder scored his first goal for the club six minutes from the end?

3. Which Arsenal player left to join Blackburn Rovers and the very next day got a hat-trick for his new club in a 4-3 win over Manchester United?

4. Arsenal's progress in the FA Cup was short lived. After beating Cardiff City 2-1 at home, they lost 1-0 at Bolton. Who was the only player to score for Arsenal in that competition?

5. Which ex-gunner scored against his old club when they lost 2-1 to West Brom at the Hawthorns on 15 October 2005?

6. It was no consolation for Arsenal that they were part of a new record when they lost 2-0 to Manchester United at Old Trafford on 9 April 2006. What was the record?

7. Who scored his first Arsenal goal in a 2-0 win at Birmingham City on 4 February 2006?

8. Why might Thierry Henry have been extra pleased when he scored in a 3-0 win over Blackburn Rovers at Highbury on 26 November 2005?

9. Which club did Arsenal beat 3-0 away in both the Premier League and the League Cup in the 2005/06 season?

10. Arsenal's 4-2 win in Highbury's final game gave the club a Champions League place for the next season at the expense of which club who missed out?

QUIZ No. 26

ARSENAL - SEASON 2006/07

1. Manchester United were Premier League winners but which club edged Arsenal out of third place on goal difference?

2. Home form in their new ground was solid. In 22 matches played in domestic competitions at The Emirates they lost just once, on 7 April 2007. It came against another club from London whose winning goal was scored by an ex-Spurs player. Who beat them and who scored?

3. Which Arsenal midfielder was the only man to be on the pitch at some point in every league game?

4. Arsenal scored ten times from the penalty spot during the Premier League campaign. Henry got three, with Adebayor and Van Persie claiming one apiece. Who was responsible for the other five, including two in one game against Spurs?

5. Ex-Gunner Nicolas Anelka scored home and away against Arsenal in the league, but for which club?

6. Despite 1989's memories, Anfield has always been a tough gig for Arsenal. However, in 2006/07 Arsenal did something on that ground that no side had done before when they won there in both domestic cup competitions, scoring nine times into the bargain. No side had knocked Liverpool out of both cups in the same season. In their 3-1 FA Cup win there on 6 January 2007, who scored two of Arsenal's goals?

7. It wasn't all plain sailing at Anfield. Liverpool beat Arsenal 4-1 when they met in the league there, made worse by which Liverpool player's hat-trick?

8. Arsenal had a great run to the League Cup Final where they lost a bad-tempered match to Chelsea. Which two Arsenal players were sent off as the game drew to its ugly close?

9. The highlight of the season was the 6-3 win at Anfield in the League Cup by a team of well-organised youngsters eager to shine, who broke through the Liverpool rearguard at will. Who was Arsenal's four-goal hero on the night?

10. Which Lancastrian club eventually removed Arsenal from that season's League Cup?

QUIZ No. 27

ARSENAL - SEASON 2007/08

1. After looking possible title winners at one point, Arsenal eventually had to settle for third spot with 83 points, the highest number for a third-placed club over a 38-match league programme. Which Arsenal defender was on the pitch at some point for all 38 games?

2. One of the Premier League's 20 clubs managed just one win all season, and their 11 points was a new record of the wrong sort. Arsenal showed them no mercy, beating them 5-0 at home and 6-2 away. Who were they and which Arsenal player got a hat-trick in both games?

3. Arsenal had gone unbeaten in the league until 12 December 2007, prompting thoughts of 2003/04 that were dashed on that day when they lost 2-1 to which club?

4. In the home fixture against Manchester United on 3 November 2007, Arsenal equalised in the last minute to make it 2-2. The scorer would have been relieved because he had earlier put through his own net. Who was he?

5. Which team did Arsenal knock out of both the FA Cup and League Cup during the season, 3-0 at home in the former and 2-0 at home in the latter?

6. Arsenal were involved in a great fight back on 29 March 2008 when, after being reduced to ten men when Diaby was sent off in the first half, they found themselves 2-0 down away from home on the hour, only to come back to win 3-2 at the death. Who were their frustrated opponents?

7. When Arsenal won 4-1 at Everton on 29 December 2007, which future Arsenal player was sent off for the home side?

8. Yellow cards were given out like confetti. Later visitors Chelsea and Bolton both racked up five, but which club, visiting Arsenal on the first day of the season, got the ball rolling with five of their own, before losing the game to a last-minute goal by Alexandr Hleb?

9. The season seemed to hinge on what happened in a 2-2 draw at Birmingham City on 23 February 2008. Arsenal were angry about a tackle that broke which player's leg in the third minute of the game?

10. Who scored both Arsenal goals in that fateful encounter?

QUIZ No. 28

ARSENAL - SEASON 2008/09

1. Robin Van Persie was Arsenal's top scorer in the Premier League and the FA Cup, but in the League Cup the award went to a player whose name also began with a 'V'. Who was he?

2. Arsenal were the only side to be involved in two 4-4 draws in the league that season. Which club provided the opposition when they drew 4-4 at The Emirates?

3. The other 4-4 draw that season was at Anfield against Liverpool. Who grabbed all four Arsenal goals?

4. Which Lancastrian club did Arsenal knock out of the FA Cup 3-0 at The Emirates, but lose to 2-0 away in the League Cup?

5. Arsenal beat another Lancashire club, who are not best mates with the answer to the previous question, 4-0 both home and away in the Premier League that season. Who were they?

6. During the season, Arsenal's four successive league games against Spurs, West Ham, Sunderland and Fulham between 31 January and 28 February all ended up with the same scoreline. What was it?

7. The player whose career was threatened by the broken leg he sustained at Birmingham in the previous season made a welcome return when he scored twice in a fourth-round FA Cup replay at The Emirates that Arsenal won 4-0. Who were they playing?

8. Which ex-Arsenal man scored against the Gunners in a 1-1 draw at Middlesbrough on 13 December 2008?

9. A fair few players have left Arsenal for Manchester United over the years, but it is extremely rare for someone to go the other way. This was rectified somewhat when Arsenal signed Mikael Silvestre, but fans struggled to remember who was the last player before him to make that journey. Who was it?

10. Nicolas Anelka came back to haunt Arsenal yet again on 10 May 2009 at The Emirates when he scored against them with yet another club, making it three clubs in all. Which team was he playing for on this occasion when they beat Arsenal 4-1?

QUIZ No. 29

ARSENAL - SEASON 2009/10

1. The season started with a bang on 15 August when Arsenal ruined that artificial confidence which home supporters entertain when that eagerly awaited first home game arrives. It was at Goodison Park against Everton when the local support's balloon was punctured by what score?

2. Which new Arsenal central defender made his debut in that first game?

3. Van Persie was injured for much of the season, starting just 14 league games. Who was Arsenal's unlikely top league goalscorer?

4. No player managed more than one goal in the two domestic cup competitions in the season. In the FA Cup, after beating West Ham United at Upton Park, Arsenal succumbed 3-1 away amid arguments about fielding a weakened team. Who took advantage of the situation to knock Arsenal out?

5. They got one match further in the League Cup that season, beating West Brom and Liverpool at The Emirates, before going down 3-0 to which club?

6. Arsenal really went to town against Lancastrian clubs at The Emirates in the Premier League. They beat Wigan Athletic 4-0 before three wins by 6-2, 4-2 and 3-1 against three clubs whose names begin with the same letter. Who were they?

7. The away game at Old Trafford was, as usual, a feisty affair. On the goals front, Arsenal went down 2-1. But they did beat United on the yellow card count with how many?

8. What assistance did Wolves give the Gunners when the away side won 4-1 at Molineux on 7 November 2009?

9. The season's darkest moment was Aaron Ramsey's broken leg at Stoke on 27 February 2010. What was the result of that game?

10. On 18 April 2010, Arsenal led 2-0 in an away game with ten minutes to go, yet contrived to lose 3-2. Who beat them, and how did the Arsenal players get home afterwards?

QUIZ No. 30

ARSENAL – SEASON 2010/11

1. A frustrating season ended with the club in fourth place in the Premier League, going out of the FA Cup to Manchester United at the quarter-final stage and losing in the League Cup Final to Birmingham City, when thousands of Arsenal fans streaming into Wembley that afternoon must have counted several million chickens that were never hatched! Which club that had played in an FA Cup Final against Arsenal in the previous century did they beat 3-1 on aggregate in the semi-final to reach that League Cup Final?

2. More doom and gloom! Which club did Arsenal help make Premier League history that season when they allowed them to come back from 4-0 down to draw 4-4?

3. The season had got off to a great start when they won their first home game 6-0, a goals margin that would be equalled but not surpassed that season. Who did they beat, and which new forward got off the mark for Arsenal?

4. Who scored all three Arsenal goals when they beat Wigan 3-0 at The Emirates in the Premier League on 22 January 2011?

5. During that season, three Arsenal players were sent off in the dying embers of games. They came at home to Birmingham City and Newcastle United, and, in the new year, at home to Manchester City. Who were the three culprits?

6. Two Fabregas penalties were crucial to Arsenal's FA Cup progress. In the third round his 90th-minute spot kick earned them a replay that they won, and then, in the fourth round, he got the winner from the spot four minutes from the end. Which two Yorkshire clubs were beaten?

7. Who was top scorer in both domestic cup competitions that season?

8. Who got Arsenal's winning goal against Manchester United on 1 May 2011?

9. The following week, Arsenal experienced one of those all-too-familiar visits to Stoke, going down 3-1. Which former Arsenal player scored one of the goals?

10. Which Arsenal winger who came off the bench 12 times in the league nevertheless appeared on the pitch at some stage of every match bar one during the season?

ARSENAL - SEASON 2011/12

1. A season of ups and downs, it ended with Arsenal in third place in the Premier League. You could call the gap between Arsenal and the two Manchester clubs that contested the title a chasm. How many points were they short of that pair?

2. The season was a great personal success for Robin Van Persie. He was on the pitch in every league game and, on 19 November, his two goals that gave Arsenal a 2-1 win at Norwich meant that he was the third player in Premier League history to score 30 goals in a calendar year. Who were the other two?

3. During the season, one aspect of the ups and downs already referred to consisted of Arsenal being the only team in the Premier League to concede eight goals in a game and score seven themselves in another. Which two teams were involved?

4. Arsenal failed at the third hurdle in both domestic cup competitions. The two sides that knocked them out met each other in a League Cup Final two years down the road. Who were they?

5. In the FA Cup fourth round that season Arsenal were struggling 2-0 down at home before two Van Persie penalties and a goal from Walcott in eight thrilling second-half minutes transformed events on the pitch. Which club lost a game they thought they were going to win?

6. Arsenal made their worst start to a league season since 1953/54 that year. Which new recruit to the forward line was sent off on his debut on the opening day in a 0-0 draw at Newcastle?

7. Certainly the most exciting game coincided with a superb Arsenal performance when, on 29 October 2011, a Van Persie hat-trick sent their fans home with broad smiles on their faces having beaten Chelsea at Stamford Bridge. What was the score?

8. Which Arsenal player scored at both ends in a 1-1 home draw with Fulham on 26 November 2011?

9. With considerable help from the home goalkeeper, by winning 3-2 at West Brom on the last day of the season, Arsenal became the top London club for the first time since which season?

10. Which man, whose association with the club went back 44 years, retired at the end of the season?

QUIZ No. 32

ARSENAL - SEASON 2012/13

1. Arsenal qualified for the Champions League for the 16th consecutive year, edging out Spurs for fourth place. The season had started promisingly with a 2-0 win at Anfield on 2 September 2012. Remind you of anything? Their two goals came from players scoring for the club for the first time. Santi Cazorla was one. Who was the other?

2. They went out of both domestic cups to clubs beginning with the same letter, one from Lancashire and the other from Yorkshire. In the FA Cup that year their 1-0 defeat at home constituted the first time Arsene Wenger had been knocked out by a side from a lower division, and in the League Cup they lost on penalties after a 1-1 draw away from home to a team that reached the final. Who were the two teams?

3. Arsenal's top scorer in the league had quite a season. He got a hat-trick against Newcastle United, the late winner in the FA Cup at Brighton, and scored the fastest Premier League goal of the season after 20 seconds at QPR. Who was he?

4. Who returned to the Arsenal team after 17 months out with injury on 27 October 2012 in the home game with QPR?

5. On 3 November 2012, at half-time in Arsenal's game with Manchester United, which Arsenal player received considerable flak for asking for ex-Gunner Van Persie's Manchester United shirt?

6. The home game with Spurs on 17 November 2012 was full of incident, with Arsenal coming back from two-goals down to win the game. Which ex-Arsenal player scored against them before being sent off, and which Arsenal defender scored his first goal for the club in the game?

7. Whose miss from the penalty spot in the last minute of the home game with Fulham allowed the visitors to leave with a point from a 3-3 draw?

8. Who scored a hat-trick for Arsenal in a 5-2 win in the Premier League at Reading in December that year?

9. Which left-sided Arsenal defender scored his first goal for the club on 16 March 2013 in a 2-0 win at Swansea?

10. Tomas Rosicky had scored just once in his last 65 Arsenal games, although to be fair it was a winning goal against Spurs. However, he got both goals on 6 April 2013 when Arsenal held on for a 2-1 away win after Per Mertesacker was sent off. Who did they beat?

ARSENAL – SEASON 2013/14

1. In winning the FA Cup in 2014, Arsenal secured their first trophy for nine years, but the opening league game produced a rather different reaction from fans when, after Koscielny was sent off, they lost 3-1 at home to which club?

2. As well as accounting for Spurs on the way to Wembley to face Hull City, Arsenal also knocked out both Merseyside clubs. One of Arsenal's scorers in the 2-1 fifth-round win over Liverpool later joined that club, while one of the scorers in the 4-1 sixth-round win over Everton was scoring against his old club. Who were the two players?

3. Mesut Ozil, Arsenal's record signing, made his debut on 14 September 2013 at The Emirates, and set up Arsenal's first goal in a 3-1 win. The visiting manager was sent to the stand and ended up being sacked the following week. Who were Arsenal's opponents, and who was the manager on thin ice?

4. Which forward scored his first Arsenal goal in a 2-1 win at Swansea on 28 September 2013?

5. On 19 October 2013, Arsenal won 4-1 at home and one of their goals, scored by Jack Wilshere after nine passing exchanges, was so delightful it was shown again and again on television as an example of how the 'beautiful game' should be played. Which club were chasing shadows?

6. On 30 November 2013 Arsenal won 3-0 against Cardiff City and one of their midfielders scored twice. Who was he, and why didn't he celebrate his two goals?

7. When Arsenal lined up for their away league game at Manchester City on 14 December 2013 they had the best defensive record in the Premier League. What happened?

8. On 11 May 2014 Arsenal confirmed Norwich City's relegation with a 2-0 win at Carrow Road. Which Arsenal defender scored his first goal for the club in this game?

9. Wigan proved a tough nut to crack in the FA Cup semi-final that season and were only beaten on penalties after a 1-1 draw after extra time. Which Arsenal player gave away the penalty from which Wigan scored, but then made amends by coming up with the equaliser?

10. In the FA Cup Final that season Arsenal were shaken by Hull's start to the game and found themselves two goals behind inside eight minutes. Eventually, after extra time, they won 3-2. Who were the last club to come from two goals down in an FA Cup Final at Wembley and end up winning the cup?

QUIZ No. 34

ARSENAL - SEASON 2014/15

1. Arsenal finished third despite a poor start that season which saw them 11 points off eventual title winners Chelsea after just eight games. In the FA Cup, however, they were creating new records, firstly by reaching the final, and then by winning the trophy. How many finals had they now contested, and how many had they won after this season?

2. The same man was Arsenal's leading scorer in the Premier League, the FA Cup and the League Cup that season, despite scoring just once in the latter competition. Who was he?

3. Which £16 million man got off the mark against Aston Villa on 20 September 2014, but almost certainly got the most satisfaction from his FA Cup sixth-round winner at Old Trafford against Manchester United?

4. On 13 December 2014 Arsenal beat Newcastle United 4-1 at The Emirates. Which player celebrated his 30th birthday with two goals?

5. The following week Arsenal were denied a victory at Anfield by a goal six minutes into time added on. Which Arsenal defender had earlier opened his Arsenal account in that game against Liverpool?

6. In three games, two in the Premier League and one in the FA Cup, who did Arsenal score 12 times against without reply?

7. Which club from a lower division did Arsenal struggle to beat after an FA Cup semi-final that went to extra time?

8. Arsenal's finest performance of the season came in an away game on 18 January 2015, which they won 2-0 with goals from Cazorla and Giroud. They were praised for their tactics and looked like they had turned a corner, but in the end it proved a false dawn. Who did they beat?

9. Arsenal were involved in a strange coincidence on their way to Wembley that year. In the FA Cup fifth round they won 3-2 away against the same team they had won against on the same ground by the same score at the same stage two years previously. Who did they beat?

10. Alexis Sanchez, in the FA Cup Final against Aston Villa, became the first Chilean player to score in the FA Cup Final since which player got the winner for Newcastle United against Arsenal in the 1952 final?

QUIZ No. 35

ARSENAL – SEASON 2015/16

1. Arsenal finished second in the Premier League behind shock winners Leicester City in 2015/16. It was their highest position since which season?

2. They were the only club to do the 'double' over Leicester City, beating them 2-1 at The Emirates in the second half of the season after winning by what score at Leicester in late September of 2015?

3. Arsenal did have the satisfaction, not for the first time, of denying Spurs the bragging rights of finishing above them that year. It all came down to the last game. Arsenal did their bit with a 4-0 home win, but Spurs lost 5-1 away against ten men when a draw would have been enough. Who did Arsenal beat, and who beat Spurs?

4. Which club did Arsenal knock out of the FA Cup for the third season running that season?

5. Which club did Arsenal win at home to in the Premier League in December 2015 and then repeat the 3-1 scoreline exactly on the same ground in January in the FA Cup?

6. In the league encounter mentioned above, which Arsenal player scored at both ends?

7. Who scored his first goal for Arsenal when they won 2-0 at Everton on 19 March 2016?

8. When Arsenal reached the FA Cup quarter-final in 2016 with a fourth home draw in a row it began to look as though they had a good chance to equal a record that had stood since 1886, that of winning the FA Cup three years consecutively. It turned out to be an anti-climax as they lost the tie 2-1. Who knocked them out and whose record would they have equalled?

9. Whose hat-trick inside seven minutes either side of half time for West Ham United in a 3-3 draw at Upton Park on 9 April 2016 put paid to Arsenal's slender hopes of the league title?

10. Back to those two games with Leicester City to finish with. Who scored a hat-trick in the away game, and who got the late winner in the home game after coming on as a substitute?

QUIZ No. 36

ARSENAL - SEASON 2016/17

1. Two unfortunate things happened in this season. Firstly, by finishing fifth, Arsenal failed to qualify for the Champions League, and, secondly, they finished below Spurs after a few close shaves in recent times. When was the last season Arsenal didn't compete in the Champions League, and in which season had Spurs last finished above them?

2. Which club knocked Arsenal out of the League Cup on their own ground for the second time in three seasons but lost 5-0 at home to Arsenal in the FA Cup?

3. Which player who was on the field for Arsenal in all their Premier League games scored a hat-trick in 14 second-half minutes in a 5-1 win at West Ham United on 3 December 2016?

4. Which four clubs beginning with the same letter did Arsenal win away to that season by 2-0, 4-1 twice and 4-0?

5. The first day of 2017 produced an Arsenal goal that the media deemed came from a 'scorpion kick'. Which Arsenal player scored it in a 2-0 home win over which club?

6. A few days later Arsenal found themselves 3-0 down away from home but bounced back to draw 3-3. Who were they playing?

7. Winning the FA Cup by beating Chelsea at Wembley redeemed that season. On their way there, Arsenal knocked out two non-league clubs, not as you would expect, in the third and fourth rounds, but in the fifth and sixth. Who were the two sides punching well above their weight?

8. In that Wembley FA Cup Final, which Arsenal defender turned in a colossal performance despite having played just 37 minutes of football during the season?

9. Which team were unfortunate to lose both Premier League games to Arsenal in the season, the first decided by a stoppage time Koscielny goal that went in off his hand, and the second with a Sanchez penalty in the 98th minute?

10. After losing the first game of the season 4-3 at home to Liverpool, Arsenal went undefeated in the league until 13 December when they lost 2-1 away to which club?

QUIZ No. 37

ARSENAL – SEASON 2017/18

1. In Arsene Wenger's final season, Arsenal dropped to sixth in the Premier League for the first time under his tenure. However, they lost just twice at home to the usual suspects. Who were they?

2. Who, in addition to being on the pitch in every league game that season, scored the crucial goal against Chelsea in the two-leg League Cup semi-final?

3. Alexandre Lacazette was Arsenal's Premier League top scorer of the season, but who was the only player to score in the Premier League and both domestic cup competitions?

4. Arsene Wenger's record of never having lost in the FA Cup third round was relinquished in his final season when they went down 4-2 at which Midlands club?

5. The season's opener brought a thrilling 4-3 win at The Emirates, with Lacazette getting his first goal for the club after 90 seconds. Who were their opponents?

6. Which player who later joined Arsenal was sent off against them while playing for Chelsea in a 0-0 draw at Stamford Bridge on 17 September 2017?

7. Arsenal enjoyed playing Everton, beating them 5-2 at home and 5-1 away. The game at Goodison Park on 3 February 2018 saw Aubameyang's first Arsenal goal, a hat-trick from another Arsenal player, and the sacking of the Everton manager within a few days. Who got the hat-trick and which manager was relieved of his duties?

8. On 25 September 2017 two goals by Lacazette gave Arsenal a 2-0 win over West Bromwich Albion at The Emirates. Which visiting player broke the record held by Ryan Giggs of 632 Premier League games?

9. On April Fools' Day that season, Aubameyang had two goals to his name at The Emirates when Arsenal were awarded a penalty. Instead of grabbing the ball and getting his hat-trick, he gave it to Lacazette and let him score instead, sparking a storm from a few members of the centre-forwards' union! Who were they playing?

10. What record was created when Spurs met Arsenal in the Premier League on 10 February 2018?

QUIZ No. 38

ARSENAL - SEASON 2018/19

1. Despite putting together some good runs during the season, Unai Emery's first year as Arsenal manager ended with failure to reach fourth place, and an abject collapse in the Europa League against Chelsea. There were just two home league defeats though, the one against Manchester City coming as no surprise, but which other club won 3-2 at The Emirates?

2. Which club were Arsenal drawn against in both domestic cup competitions that season, winning 3-0 away in the FA Cup, and 2-1 at home in the League Cup?

3. Aubameyang was the season's top Premier League scorer for Arsenal, but the two men who topped the FA Cup and League Cup goal charts had names that began with the same letter. Who were they?

4. Arsenal won 5-1 away from home in the Premier League on 7 October 2018 and lost 5-1 away from home in the same competition on 29 December. Which two clubs were involved in their contrasting fortunes?

5. In the game in December 2018 that Arsenal lost 5-1 they had taken an early lead when which youngster scored his first goal for the club before the roof fell in?

6. At the beginning of December 2018, Arsenal had won the one that matters most, beating Spurs 4-2 at The Emirates. Which Arsenal midfielder endeared himself to the home crowd by scoring his first Arsenal goal?

7. A few days later, in December 2018, Arsenal went to Old Trafford and drew 2-2. The match was notable for having no Alex Ferguson in the home dugout and no Arsene Wenger in the away. How many years before that was it since Manchester United and Arsenal played each other without at least one of them being there?

8. On 16 December 2018 Arsenal's unbeaten 22-game run came to an end when they lost 3-2 away to a team that had just parted company with their manager and the visit of Arsenal coincided with the new man's first home game, never what you want to see! Who beat them?

9. Whose miss from the penalty spot in the last minute in the away game prevented Arsenal from doing the double over Spurs that season?

10. Aubameyang got two goals in a 3-1 win at Burnley on the last day of the season, and if he had put away a chance near the end he would have won the Golden Boot outright instead of having to share it with which two players?

QUIZ No. 39

ARSENAL — SEASON 2019/20

1. When Arsenal finally completed the last Premier League game of the longest, craziest season on record, how many top-flight seasons of league football had they played?

2. At the start of the season Arsenal sold a popular defender to Real Sociedad and paid Lille £72 million, a club record, for a highly talented creative midfielder, although it probably turned out that they paid £70 million for his left foot and the other £2 million for his right! Who were the two players, one leaving and one arriving?

3. A 5-0 League Cup win over Nottingham Forest that season turned out to be Unai Emery's biggest Arsenal win. Who, on his debut, opened and closed the scoring?

4. Who scored his first goal for Arsenal when they beat Bournemouth 1-0 at The Emirates in October 2019?

5. Unai Emery was sacked on 29 November 2019 after losing at home in Europe. Freddie Ljungberg was placed in temporary charge. Who was Emery's last Premier League game against and who provided the opposition for Ljungberg's first Premier League match?

6. Mikel Arteta was unveiled as the new Arsenal manager on 20 December 2019, and on Boxing Day they travelled to Bournemouth for his first game at the helm. Who was the first Arsenal player to score for the new manager in the ensuing 1-1 draw?

7. A memorable League Cup tie has been dealt with elsewhere, but who was the only Arsenal player to score in both the FA Cup and the League Cup that season?

8. Although eighth place in the Premier League was a poor effort, supporters were compensated by another FA Cup win against the odds that season. Arsenal beat two Yorkshire clubs and two from the south coast on their way to the heroics against Manchester City and Chelsea. Who were the four clubs?

9. The pandemic meant a gap of 102 days between the league game Arsenal played on 7 March 2020 and the next one on 17 June. Who was the last team Arsenal played before that long break and the first team they played when football resumed?

10. Arsenal met Norwich City in the first competitive game the club had ever played in a July, winning 4-0 at home. Who scored a great goal on his debut for the club in that game?

QUIZ No. 40

ARSENAL V SPURS - LEAGUE 1900-99

1. Arsenal and Spurs played each other in the league for the first time on 4 December 1909 when 18,000 saw Woolwich Arsenal win 1-0 with a goal by Lawrence. On which ground was the match played?

2. In 1934/35 Arsenal thrashed Spurs 5-1 at Highbury and 6-0 at White Hart Lane. Who scored five of the 11 goals?

3. On 13 March 1957 Arsenal won 3-1 at White Hart Lane with one of their players finding the net twice in the game. The odd thing about it was that this wing-half played 146 games for Arsenal and scored just two goals, both of them in the same game against Spurs! Who was he?

4. Arsenal clinched the first leg of their league and cup double in 1970/71 by winning 1-0 at White Hart Lane on the evening of 3 May 1971. Whose header was decisive with just minutes to go?

5. Why were the two derby matches with Spurs in 1990/91 unique in the history of these clashes?

6. In 1992/93, on the night of 11 May, with Arsenal due to play in the FA Cup Final four days later, George Graham put a reserve team out to face Spurs in the league at Highbury. This act divided opinion amongst Arsenal fans as they endured a 3-1 defeat. The scorer of Arsenal's goal that night scored a much more vital one for Manchester City six years later. Who was he?

7. On 23 December 1978 Arsenal recorded their biggest win at White Hart Lane since 1935 when they won 5-0. A goal with a swerving left-foot shot left John Motson's voice an octave higher as he struggled to find superlatives to describe it. Who scored it?

8. In between February 1958 and October 1963 Arsenal and Spurs produced three thrilling draws, two at Highbury and one at White Hart Lane, with the same scoreline in all three games. What was it?

9. Which legendary Arsenal centre-forward on 13 January 1955 scored the goal that beat Spurs 1-0 at White Hart Lane, it being the only time he scored for them against Spurs?

10. Who, in season 1910/11, became the first Arsenal player to score home and away against Spurs in the same season?

QUIZ No. 41

ARSENAL V SPURS – CUP COMPETITIONS – 1900-99

1. When Arsenal moved on to Tottenham territory in 1913, fans of both clubs probably wanted them to draw each other in the FA Cup as soon as possible. However, two world wars took place before it happened. When it did, Arsenal won a third-round tie 3-0 at Highbury. It was played on 8 January in what year?

2. The next time the rivals were paired against each other came in the semi-final of the League Cup in 1968/69, when over 55,000 watched each leg, with Arsenal going through 2-1 on aggregate. Who scored both their goals, the winner in a 1-0 win at Highbury and the other in a 1-1 draw at White Hart Lane?

3. They were drawn to face each other in the same competition in the fourth round in 1980/81, and this time Spurs won 1-0 with a goal from a man with a World Cup winner's medal. Who was he?

4. Spurs won the next meeting as well, in a third-round FA Cup tie at White Hart Lane on 2 January 1982 when a rare error from Arsenal's goalkeeper ended with Garth Crooks netting the winner. Who was playing in goal for Arsenal on that occasion?

5. When they next met it was a real cliff hanger over three matches in the League Cup semi-final of 1986/87, with Arsenal eventually going through after being 2-0 down on aggregate at half time in the second leg. Which ex-Arsenal player who never kicked a ball for the club scored for Spurs in all three games?

6. Two Arsenal men whose surnames begin with 'A' scored for them, one in the 2-1 extra-time win at White Hart Lane in the second leg, and the other in the third match that Arsenal won 2-1 at White Hart Lane after Spurs had won the toss for the third match venue. Who were the two scorers?

7. Which Arsenal player finally won it for them with his goal near the end of the third game that put the Gunners ahead for the first time in the marathon?

8. On 14 April 1991, although Arsenal were favourites to beat Spurs in that year's FA Cup semi-final, Gazza intervened, and they lost 3-1. Who scored their goal with a header?

9. Two years later the clubs met again at the same stage and this time Arsenal prevailed by their favourite score of 1-0. Who got the vital goal?

10. Spurs fans had likened the scorer of that goal to a beast of burden. Outside Wembley afterwards they had to endure Arsenal fans chanting five words at them. What were those five words?

QUIZ No. 42

ARSENAL V SPURS – LEAGUE 2000-20

1. How many of their 20 home league games against Spurs in this time period have Arsenal lost?

2. What is the highest number of goals Arsenal have scored in an away game at Spurs this century?

3. Who is the only player this century to score for Arsenal against Spurs and for Spurs against Arsenal in the league?

4. One scoreline has prevailed three years running at The Emirates and three years running at White Hart Lane this century. What is it?

5. Who is the only Arsenal player to score in a Premier League game against Spurs in both this century and the previous one?

6. Arsenal took Spurs to the cleaners by the same score at The Emirates two years running, in 2011/12 and 2012/13. What was that score?

7. The highest scoring draw in the game this century was 4-4. Where was it played and in which season?

8. 1-0 to the Arsenal is a familiar cry, and supporters would have been pleased with the two games against the old enemy in season 2013/14 because they won both of them by that score. Which two Arsenal players were on target, the one at White Hart Lane coming before many people were settled in their seats?

9. In 2010/11 the clubs provided an exciting 3-3 draw at White Hart Lane. Two Dutchmen, one from each side, whose names begin with the same three letters, were on the mark in the match. Who were they?

10. On 8 November 2015 Arsenal were trailing 1-0 at home to Spurs going into the final minutes when which defender slid in at the far post to save the Gunners from defeat?

QUIZ No. 43

ARSENAL V SPURS - CUP COMPETITIONS - 2000-20

1. The clubs met for the first time in a cup competition this century on 8 April 2001 in an FA Cup semi-final at Old Trafford. After Doherty had given Spurs the lead, which two Arsenal players produced the goals that turned the game in their favour?

2. They came up against each other again in the 2006/07 season in another semi-final, this time over two legs in the League Cup. Which Arsenal player was a key figure in the first leg at White Hart Lane when, after putting through his own net to give Spurs a 2-0 half-time lead, he got two goals at the right end in the second half to force a 2-2 draw?

3. The second leg in the 2006/07 League Cup went to extra-time after a 1-1 draw at The Emirates, Arsenal finally going through 3-1 on the night and 5-3 on aggregate. Which two players with names beginning with the same letter scored for them that night?

4. Arsenal met Spurs yet again in the same competition the following year at the same stage when the first leg at The Emirates finished 1-1. Who scored Arsenal's goal?

5. The second leg was something of a disaster for Arsenal, who were taken apart 5-1 at White Hart Lane. Which Arsenal player summed the night up perfectly by putting through his own net and coming close to a punch up with another Arsenal player?

6. Yet again it was the League Cup that provided the excuse for another local derby in 2010/11 when, on 21 September, Arsenal won 4-1 after extra-time in the third round at White Hart Lane. Whose two goals from the penalty spot in extra-time saw them home?

7. It was the same story on 23 September 2015 in another third-round League Cup meeting at White Hart Lane. Which midfielder came up with both goals in Arsenal's 2-1 win?

8. Which Arsenal defender was unfortunate enough to score the Spurs goal in that game by putting through his own net?

9. Not long before Christmas in 2018, Spurs exacted some revenge by winning a League Cup quarter-final at The Emirates by what score?

10. By 2020, Arsenal and Spurs had both played in eight League Cup finals. Who were the only club to beat both of them in a League Cup Final?

QUIZ No. 44

ARSENE'S ASIDES

1. About whose reaction to an incident with Adebayor of Manchester City did Wenger say: 'If someone stamps on your head in that way you wouldn't say "Thank you very much" and turn the other cheek. Only Jesus Christ did that'?

2. About which manager did Wenger say: 'His remarks are out of order, disconnected from reality and disrespectful. When you give success to stupid people it sometimes makes them more stupid'?

3. About which club's pursuit of Thierry Henry did Wenger say: 'I want to buy Buckingham Palace but that doesn't mean to say that I can have it'?

4. On which manager's tardiness in apologising did Wenger say: 'If there is an apology it must be coming by horseback'?

5. On which player's loan back to Spain in 2007 did Wenger say: 'Despite global warming England is still not warm enough for him.'?

6. What is the missing word at the end of this Wenger quote: Talking about fan unrest, 'We won the double for them last season and when you taste caviar it's difficult to go back to _____.'?

7. About the signing of which young player did Wenger say: 'We even watched him in training. How did I do that? With a hat and a moustache'?

8. What idea had the egregious Blatter put forward when Wenger said: 'It's unbelievable. Maybe Mr Blatter drunk too much champagne to welcome in the new year'?

9. After a heavy defeat against which club did Wenger say the following, and why was it particularly galling for him: 'I take full responsibility. We got a good kicking, it's one of the worst days of my career. The best way is not to explain too much the mistakes.'?

10. About which non-Arsenal player did Wenger say: 'He's the biggest English talent I've seen since I took over at Highbury'?

QUIZ No. 45

ASSORTED GUNNERS - PART 1

1. If this current Arsenal defender was caught doing this in his own penalty area he might well give away a spot kick. Who is he?

2. Some players like to say they are 'over the moon' when they score, but this player seems to go beyond that, particularly to describe a vital winner he got at Old Trafford. Who was he?

3. He played 86 league games for the club between 1935 and 1946 in a war-affected career. His surname is the name of the famous wife of a 1960s Arsenal manager. Who was he?

4. He played 25 times in the league up front for Arsenal between 1997 and 1999. It sounds like a dead snake may be involved here! Who was he?

5. Arsenal's only palindromic player, who scored 17 goals for the club in 46 outings between 1897 and 1899. He shares his name with the only palindromic player to score in an FA Cup Final, who did so for Newcastle United in 1955. Who was the Arsenal player?

6. He came from Liverpool in 1991 and left for Portsmouth in 1995 after 25 league games and two goals to his name. He shares his full name with a president of the United States. Who was he?

7. He started out in the forward line, but eventually switched to midfield, making 220 league appearances between 1948 and 1960, scoring 51 times. He shares his name with places in both West Sussex and South Oxfordshire. Who was he?

8. Who is the only Arsenal player to share his surname with two presidents of the United States?

9. This Arsenal left-back who played 253 times for the club between 1958 and 1966 was called 'Flint' by the fans, although his real name was Bill. Who was he and why did they call him 'Flint'?

10. General Custer was killed at the battle of Little Big Horn in 1876. His first two names together produce one of the most popular players in Arsenal's history. Who?

QUIZ No. 46

ASSORTED GUNNERS – PART 2

1. Which two post-war England internationals who collectively played for the club 630 times in all competitions share an occupation as a surname that is a different word in each case, but means broadly the same thing?

2. He's an area of London and a celebrated guitarist who was capped once for England on 26 November 1958 in a 2-2 draw at Villa Park. It was an afternoon game that was shown live on TV, a rarity at the time. Who was he?

3. He played 94 times on the wing for Arsenal in all competitions, scoring 16 goals between 1949 and 1953, and is still required between Putney and Mortlake in April each year. Who was he?

4. You would have to ask him whether he considered his Arsenal career to be 'days of wine and roses', but he was at the heart of Arsenal's defence between 1974 and 1976 on 62 occasions, scoring one goal, a winner against Wolves in April 1976. Who was he?

5. Key members of the 1970/71 'double' team, which two players shared their surname with a president of the United States?

6. The uncle played for Arsenal over 200 times between 1955 and 1964, and the nephew played for them around the same amount between 1986 and 1992, notably coming off the bench an amazing 83 times. Who were they?

7. Which famous Arsenal player from the 1920s shared his surname with the author of *The 39 Steps* spy thriller?

8. Sam Bartram, the unluckiest goalkeeper not to win an England cap, played over 600 games for Charlton Athletic in a legendary career. Arsenal had their own goalkeeper called Bartram who played 12 times for them between 1994 and 1997. What was his first name?

9. Which playing card, who turned out for Arsenal over 200 times, scored in two FA Cup finals for another club in the inter-war years?

10. We have no record of whether this Arsenal defender disliked playing in the middle of March, but it's just possible that was the case. He played 50 times for the club before joining Cambridge United in 1991. Who was he?

QUIZ No. 47

BIRTHPLACES

1. Three Arsenal frontmen of different generations, David Jack, Tommy Lawton and Paul Mariner, all came from the same Lancashire town. Which one?

2. Which Spanish town well known for an annual event in its streets do Manuel Almunia and Nacho Monreal hail from?

3. Arsenal players Viv Anderson, Jermaine Pennant and Andy Cole were all born in which city?

4. Which one of these former Arsenal players was not born in Swansea? – Mel Charles, Ray Daniel, John Hartson, Jack Kelsey or Aaron Ramsey?

5. Which Dutch city were Gianni Van Bronkhurst and Robin Van Persie born in?

6. Which two post-war Arsenal goalkeepers were born in Chesterfield?

7. Here are seven Scottish Arsenal players. Three come from Glasgow, another three from Edinburgh, while the other one was born in Ayr. Which one was he? – Tommy Docherty, Jimmy Logie, Peter Marinello, Frank McLintock, Charlie Nicholas, Ian Ure and Willie Young.

8. Here are four Arsenal players and four geographical locations. Can you match them up with their birthplace? – Alex Oxlade-Chamberlain, John Hollins, Theo Walcott and Martin Keown with Guildford, Oxford, Portsmouth and Newbury.

9. David O'Leary, the man who holds the Arsenal appearances record, was born in an area of London that contains the name of a football club in its title. Where was he born?

10. As he's known as the 'Romford Pele', it's not hard to work out Ray Parlour's origins, and goalkeeper Stuart Taylor also comes from that neck of the woods. But which legendary Arsenal player was also born there?

QUIZ No. 48

CHRISTMAS CRACKERS

1. On Christmas Day 1894, Woolwich Arsenal won 7-0 at home. If Robbie Williams had been alive then it might just have put him off his Christmas dinner! Who did they beat?

2. Another very satisfying Christmas for Arsenal came on Boxing Day of 1983 when two goals each for Charlie Nicholas and Raphael Meade saw them to a 4-2 away win against which club?

3. It has not always been good cheer at Yuletide for Arsenal. On Boxing Day 1910 and Christmas Day 1911 they lost heavily by the same score at Manchester United and Spurs. What was that score?

4. In the first Christmas of the new millennium Arsenal, assisted by a Thierry Henry hat-trick, had a 6-1 Boxing Day victory at Highbury against which Midlands club?

5. One Arsenal player certainly loved Christmas, scoring on three successive Boxing Days as well as on the day after Boxing Day the following year. All this happened between 1972 and 1975. Who was he?

6. On Christmas Day 1896 Woolwich Arsenal won 6-2 against a team they went on to lose to 5-0 on Christmas Day three years later. This team shares their name with an American car. Who were they?

7. I don't expect many Arsenal fans were in Lancashire on Christmas Day in 1952 to see them beat which club in a 6-4 thriller?

8. It was Christmas Eve in 1932 when that free-scoring Arsenal side ruined Sheffield United's Christmas at Highbury. There were 11 goals in the game. How many of them did Arsenal score?

9. Arsenal made the long trek to the North East on 28 December 1935, losing 5-4 to which club?

10. You have to laugh when modern players say they aren't in the right
    frame of mind to play while picking up astronomic sums. You had
    to be in the right frame of mind back then, and Arsenal certainly
    were for Christmas of 1930. They won 4-1 at Manchester City, 3-1
    at home to the same club, and 7-1 at home to Blackpool in the space
    of how many festive days?

QUIZ No. 49

CRICKETING CONNECTIONS

Identify the Arsenal players whose names have links with the summer game.

1. To play cricket you definitely need one of these. 177 league games, 45 goals, 1971–76.

2. And this is what it is made of. Eight league games, goalkeeper, 1896–98.

3. Goalkeeper who won medals with West Ham United and topped the bowling averages in 1964 with Worcestershire. 35 games, 1952–60.

4. Bowlers like rubbing this into the ball on occasion. Seven games, no goals, 1912–19.

5. Test cricketer whose batting in the summer of 1947 was of a verve and quality rarely glimpsed before or since. 54 games, 15 goals, 1932–50.

6. The last man to be capped by England at both football and cricket. 75 games, 18 goals, 1945–55.

7. His brother captained England at the game with the smaller ball. 58 games, five goals, 1974–81.

8. They used to wear this colour to play cricket before the game was reduced to trying to hit the ball out of the ground in coloured pyjamas! 101 games, 40 goals, 1919–23.

9. West Indian spin bowler, the first such to take 300 Test wickets. 137 games, two goals, 2007–17.

10. Cricketing term based on superstition that's mentioned when a player or team has 111 or multiples of it. 255 games, 10 goals, 1966–81.

QUIZ No. 50

CUP CAPTAINS

Can you name the Arsenal captain for each of these winning finals?

1. Arsenal 2 Huddersfield Town 0 – FA Cup – 1930

2. Arsenal 1 Sheffield United 0 – FA Cup – 1936

3. Arsenal 2 Liverpool 0 – FA Cup – 1950

4. Arsenal 2 Liverpool 1 – FA Cup – 1971

5. Arsenal 3 Manchester United 2 – FA Cup – 1979

6. Arsenal 2 Liverpool 1 – League Cup – 1987

7. Arsenal 2 Newcastle United 0 – FA Cup 1998

8. Arsenal 1 Southampton 0 – FA Cup – 2003

9. Arsenal 0 Manchester United 0 (won on penalties) – FA Cup – 2005

10. Arsenal 4 Aston Villa 0 – FA Cup – 2015

QUIZ No. 51

THE EMIRATES - PART 1

1. The previous use of the land on which Arsenal built their new ground certainly gave supporters of other clubs the opportunity for some amusement at their expense. What had it been?

2. Some supporters who weren't pleased with the new ground's name being linked to a corporate identity still call it by its original name. What was it?

3. UEFA regulations mean that it can't be called 'The Emirates Stadium' for European competitions. What is it called when Arsenal play home games in Europe?

4. It would have been fitting if the first competitive goal in the stadium had been scored by an Arsenal player, but there's always someone who wants to gatecrash your party. On its opening game who were the visitors who drew 1-1 on 19 August 2006, and which player from that club scored that first goal?

5. What links the first league game, the first FA Cup tie and the first League Cup game in the new stadium?

6. What was the costing figure for the ground in 2004?
   (a) £190 million (b) £290 million (c) £390 million (d) £490 million

7. Who got Arsenal's equaliser on 19 August 2006?

8. Which three players' contributions to the club have been recognised by statues outside the ground?

9. Who were Arsenal's first opponents in an FA Cup tie at The Emirates?

10. A company called Populous were the main one involved in the construction of the new ground. Which racecourse had they previously redeveloped in 2005?

QUIZ No. 52

THE EMIRATES - PART 2

1. Which Arsenal player ceremonially installed the first seat in the new ground on 13 March 2006?

2. The ground was officially opened on 26 October 2006 by someone acting as a substitute for the original person who was indisposed. Who were the two people involved?

3. Which club did Arsenal beat to reach their first domestic cup final while playing on their new ground?

4. Which country, rather absurdly, played eight international matches at The Emirates between 2006 and 2018?

5. Given the trend for multi-purpose stadia, which American rock star was the first to play The Emirates in a concert on 30 May 2008?

6. In which year does 'The Emirates' naming rights to the stadium run out?

7. What is the official capacity of the stadium?
   (a) 60,704 (b) 61,704 (c) 62,704 (d) 63,704

8. There are only two league clubs in the UK with a higher capacity. Who are they?

9. Arsenal employ a problematic procedure when issuing attendance statistics. They count tickets sold rather than 'bums on seats', which paints a rosier picture than might actually be the case. Bate Borisov visited The Emirates for a Europa League game on 7 December 2017 when the official attendance was given as 54,648. Those monitoring the game suggested the real figure was just less than what?
   (a) 26,000 (b) 31,000 (c) 36,000 (d) 41,000

10. Who were Arsenal playing on 3 November 2007 when the attendance record at the new stadium was broken with a crowd of 60,161?

QUIZ No. 53

FA CUP FINALS - CLUBS

1. Who are the only club that Arsenal have beaten in three FA Cup finals?

2. Who are the only club Arsenal beat more than once in a 20th-century FA Cup Final?

3. Who are the only club to have beaten Arsenal in more than one FA Cup Final?

4. Which three clubs in beating Arsenal in an FA Cup Final were registering their sole win in the competition?

5. Who are the only London club to beat Arsenal in an FA Cup Final?

6. Which three Yorkshire clubs have Arsenal defeated in an FA Cup Final?

7. Arsenal have been in an FA Cup Final replay just once. Who was it against?

8. Arsenal have scored four goals in an FA Cup Final just once. Who were they playing?

9. Who are the only four clubs to score more than once in an FA Cup Final against Arsenal?

10. One club from outside the top flight have lost an FA Cup Final to Arsenal. Who are they?

QUIZ No. 54

FA CUP FINALS - PLAYERS

1. Which three men have scored for Arsenal in more than one FA Cup Final, not counting replays?

2. If you take the scorer of Arsenal's goal against Newcastle United in the 1932 FA Cup Final and add the scorer of their two goals against Liverpool in the 1950 FA Cup Final, you should come up with a well-known department store. What is it?

3. Whose injury in the 1952 FA Cup Final against Newcastle United rendered him a 'passenger'? Despite a spirited display Arsenal lost the match.

4. Arsenal signed two players from the Ipswich Town team that had beaten them in the 1978 FA Cup Final, one of them appearing and scoring for them in the FA Cup Final of 1979. Who were the two players?

5. Which is the only racecourse to score against Arsenal in an FA Cup Final?

6. This has got to be hard to take. This player left Blackpool for Everton, and when he arrived he saw the FA Cup in their trophy cabinet. After a losing final for Everton in 1968 against West Brom, he moved to Arsenal, and there was that trophy again sitting there on the sideboard at Highbury, won by Arsenal before his arrival. In the following season he reached the final with them but lost to Leeds United. Then he moved to Southampton, and, lo and behold, there was that trophy again laughing at him. He never did win it! Who was he?

7. Which two players with names beginning with 'H' have scored against Arsenal in an FA Cup Final?

8. If you reverse the number 10 and number 11 in Arsenal's line up in the 1971 FA Cup Final against Liverpool you produce an actor who won an Oscar for his performance alongside Paul Newman in the 1967 film *Cool Hand Luke*. Who was he?

9. Which three central-defenders have scored for Arsenal in an FA Cup Final or replay?

10. Who are the only two players with names starting with a 'P' to score for Arsenal in an FA Cup Final?

QUIZ No. 55

FANS

1. Which Cumbrian novelist and television arts presenter has been an Arsenal fan for many years?

2. Which golfer with an amazing Ryder Cup record is an Arsenal fan?

3. Astronomer and Arsenal fan Ian P. Griffin has named what 33179 Arsenewenger?

4. In the world of horse racing, two of the biggest names in the sport are keen Arsenal fans. One is a retired jumps jockey who dominated that game for 20 years, and the other is a very successful flat jockey who has won the Arc de Triomphe more times than any other jockey. Who are they?

5. Apparently, this singer from London is 'no angel', but she's still a big Arsenal fan. Who is she?

6. Which head of state was a keen Arsenal fan from 1971 onwards and was hoping to attend Arsenal's away game with Auxerre in the European Cup Winners' Cup quarter-final on 16 March 1995 but was prevented from doing so at the last minute by his security people?

7. Which actor, who played the doctor who wanted his sausages whatever the risk in *Fawlty Towers*, was a regular at The Emirates?

8. Which Eastenders actor wrote a book about his experiences on Highbury's North Bank in the 1990s?

9. Two Americans, one a film director and the other a rapper, are alleged to be Arsenal fans. Who are they?

10. Rock musicians are a good source for Arsenal fans. Apparently both Mick Jagger and Roger Daltrey are fond of the Gunners, while we are told that as many as two members of Pink Floyd support them. It's probably the only thing they were in agreement about! Who are they?

QUIZ No. 56

FOOTBALLER OF THE YEAR

1. Who, in 1950, was the first Arsenal player to win the Football Writers' Association 'Footballer of the Year' award?

2. Who, in 1979, was the first Arsenal player to win the Professional Footballers' Association 'Footballer of the Year' award?

3. Two Arsenal players won the Scottish 'Footballer of the Year' award with Celtic, one in 1983 before his spell at Highbury, and the other in 2005 after his time at the club. Who were the two players?

4. Which member of Arsenal's double-winning side of 1971 received the FWA 'Footballer of the Year' award that year?

5. Who was the only Arsenal player to win either of the top two awards in the 1990s?

6. Which two Arsenal players won the 'Young Player of the Year' award in the 1980s, one in 1987 and the other in 1989?

7. Who was the first Arsenal player to win the FWA award this century when he took it in 2002?

8. Which Arsenal player is the only man to win the FWA award three times?

9. Which Arsenal player won both the FWA and PFA awards in 2012?

10. Which two Arsenal players have won the 'Young Player of the Year' award this century, the first in 2008 and the second in 2011?

QUIZ No. 57

GOALKEEPERS - PART 1

1. Who played in goal for Arsenal when they beat Chelsea in the 2017 FA Cup Final?

2. Who is the only Arsenal goalkeeper to be sent off in a European final?

3. Which Arsenal goalkeeper, who shared his full name with a member of Pink Floyd, made 22 appearances for the club in the early years of this century?

4. After 146 appearances for Arsenal between 1974 and 1977 he moved to Aston Villa, where his dramatic injury at the start of the 1982 European Cup Final meant he could take no further part in the greatest night in Villa's history. Who was he?

5. Who played over 350 times between the sticks for Arsenal between 1949 and 1962 while gaining 41 Welsh caps?

6. A dependable goalkeeper who joined Arsenal from Bradford City in 1936 and finished up playing just short of 300 games for the club in a career badly affected by the war. Who was he?

7. Arsenal have had two goalkeepers with the same surname play for them in FA Cup finals. What is that surname?

8. He played 157 times for Arsenal between 1931 and 1937 before becoming Hearts manager. You won't find him hanging around with the likes of Mick Jagger or Keith Richards! Who was he?

9. Legend has it that the new, unwashed jersey he played in was responsible for his error that cost Arsenal the 1927 FA Cup Final against Cardiff City. Being Welsh probably didn't help either! However, he went on to play 167 games for the Gunners. Who was he?

10. Which Spanish club did Arsenal obtain Manuel Almunia from?

QUIZ No. 58

GOALKEEPERS - PART 2

1. Who played in goal for Arsenal in the 1972 FA Cup Final against Leeds United?

2. Which Arsenal goalkeeper from the mid-1960s, who shares his surname with a well-known poet, also played for three other London clubs, namely Crystal Palace, Charlton Athletic and Brentford?

3. Which Arsenal goalkeeper joined the club having already won a Champions League winners' medal?

4. From which German club did Arsenal buy Bernd Leno?

5. David Seaman spent time at five other clubs during his career. Which was the only one he played over 100 league games for?

6. Which Argentinian goalkeeper, who was on Arsenal's books for several years before getting a chance to show what he could do, finally got that chance in the 2019/20 season, but was promptly sold to Aston Villa?

7. Which Polish Arsenal goalkeeper won an FA Cup winners' medal with the club against Aston Villa in 2015? A bonus point if you spell it correctly!

8. Which two Arsenal goalkeepers have appeared in three successive FA Cup finals for the club?

9. Arsenal's goalkeeper in the 2014 FA Cup Final against Hull City has a surname nine letters long. The first six produce a 1960s pop star, and the last three is what some folks like to do when there's a bit of snow lying around! Who was he?

10. He was at Arsenal between 1997 and 2002 and played 63 games in all competitions, but he made an indelible impression on me when he took over from an injured David Seaman and helped Arsenal do the 'double'. Like a racehorse he seemed inexplicably to lose his form later in his career, but for those games up to the end of the 1997/98 season he made a colossal impact, particularly in a vital FA Cup replay at Upton Park where he performed miracles. Who was he?

QUIZ No. 59

GREENER GRASS

1. Which player who appeared more than 100 times for Arsenal won an FA Cup winners' medal with Everton in 1995?

2. Scoring for Liverpool in the 1992 FA Cup Final win over Sunderland hardly made up for what he had inflicted on the Anfield club earlier on in his career with Arsenal. Who was he?

3. Which three ex-Arsenal players were part of the Portsmouth team that won the FA Cup in 2008?

4. Which two Arsenal centre-forwards moved to Old Trafford and scored for them in an FA Cup Final, one in the 1960s and the other in the 1980s?

5. Which ex-Arsenal player was in the Liverpool team that won the FA Cup for the first time in 1965?

6. Which ex-Arsenal player managed to get on the field in time added on in the 2011 FA Cup Final for Manchester City against Stoke City?

7. Which two ex-Arsenal players were in the Chelsea side that won the FA Cup in 2009 and 2010?

8. Which three ex-Arsenal players couldn't stop Wigan Athletic from bringing a smile to the face of football by beating Manchester City in the 2013 FA Cup Final?

9. Which ex-Arsenal player sat on the bench for Crystal Palace against Manchester United in the 2016 FA Cup Final without getting on?

10. Which two ex-Arsenal players were in the Chelsea team that won the 2018 FA Cup Final against Manchester United?

QUIZ No. 60

HAT-TRICKS

1. Which Arsenal wide man got three goals against Middlesbrough in a 5-1 win at Highbury in the Premier League on 20 November 1999?

2. On 5 November 2001 whose hat-trick was a significant contribution to the 4-0 defeat of Manchester United in a League Cup tie at Highbury?

3. Which Arsenal front man grabbed two league hat-tricks before Christmas in 1993 in 4-0 wins at home to Ipswich Town and away to Swindon Town?

4. In the UEFA Cup of 1999/2000 a 4-2 away win against Werder Bremen brought a rare hat-trick for which popular Arsenal midfielder?

5. Which Arsenal player scored a hat-trick in a 6-0 win over Sheffield United in a League Cup tie at The Emirates in 2008?

6. Which Arsenal midfielder scored all of the goals in a 3-0 home win over Manchester City in the league on 23 April 1983?

7. It's a rare thing for two players from the same club to get a hat-trick in the same game, but this was what happened when Arsenal beat Staevnet 7-1 in the Inter- Cities Fairs Cup in the 1963/64 season. Which two players shared six of the seven goals?

8. On 9 December 2015 Arsenal went to Olympiakos knowing they had to win to progress from the group stage of the Champions League. Whose hat-trick saw them through 3-0?

9. On 19 October 2016 Arsenal won 6-0 at home against Ludogorets in the group stage of the Champions League. Who scored a second-half hat-trick in the game?

10. On 6 December of that same year another less well-known Arsenal player got a hat-trick in the group stage in a 4-1 away win against Basle. Who was he?

QUIZ No. 61

HIGHBURY

1. Mired in controversy when Arsenal moved there in 1913, it eventually became a shrine to supporters for the best part of a century. Which august authority figure had to put his signature to the document allowing Arsenal to lease the land?

2. Arsenal opened the 1913/14 season in their new ground with a Second Division match there on 6 September, with George Jobey having the honour of being the first goalscorer in a 2-1 win over which club from the Midlands?

3. Highbury was regularly used by the national team, beginning with a 2-1 defeat when Wales beat England on 15 March 1920. Which future Arsenal player scored England's first goal at the ground?

4. Highbury was in the news on 14 November 1934 when England won an ill-tempered affair by 3-2 against Italy. Arsenal created a record for the number of players provided for England by a league club. How many of the XI came from the club?

5. In the 1930s Herbert Chapman persuaded the London Underground to rename the nearest tube station 'Arsenal'. What had it previously been called?

6. Who is the only Arsenal player to score a hat-trick for England at Highbury? It came in a 6-2 win over Hungary on 2 December 1936.

7. Which legendary centre-forward, who ended his career at Arsenal in the mid-1950s, was the only player to score from the penalty spot for England at Highbury when he converted in a 4-2 win over Sweden on 18 November 1947?

8. Which Arsenal full-back was their only contribution to the England team that beat France 3-0 in Highbury's first international after the war on 3 May 1947?

9. The curtain came down on the old place on that emotional day of 7 May 2006. Whose hat-trick helped memorialise the day?

10. Wigan Athletic were the visitors on that day, going down in fitting fashion by 4-2. But which club played Arsenal in Highbury's last-ever cup tie?

QUIZ No. 62

HIGHBURY HEROES – No.1 – TONY ADAMS

1. In what two ways does the number 66 figure in the life of Tony Adams? Hopefully he didn't catch the number 66 bus up to Highbury in the early 80s!

2. Tony Adams has achieved two remarkable records involving three different decades, one in club football and the other in international football. What are they?

3. Against which club did Tony Adams make his Arsenal debut on 5 November 1983 at Highbury?

4. On which away ground did Tony Adams score his first Arsenal goal on 30 August 1986?

5. In Tony Adams's testimonial in May 2002 at Highbury, the game ended in a 1-1 draw. Who provided the opposition, and which Arsenal player scored their goal in his last ever outing for the Gunners?

6. Tony Adams scored five goals for England, the first of which came on 11 November 1987 in a 4-1 win in an away European qualifier against a country that political change has now rendered non-existent. Who were they?

7. When Tony Adams also scored in a 2-0 win over Ukraine on 31 May 2000, what was special about his goal?

8. When he retired and moved into management, why was it appropriate that Tony Adams became the manager of Wycombe Wanderers?

9. When Tony Adams took over the role of caretaker manager at Portsmouth, Arsene Wenger, his old boss, apparently said, 'welcome to hell'. He shared this hell with another battle-hardened tough guy who has since been involved with another club in North London. Who was he?

10. In his 665 Arsenal appearances in all competitions did Tony Adams score more or less than 50 goals?

QUIZ No. 63

HIGHBURY HEROES –
No.2 – DENNIS BERGKAMP

1. Despite a problem with the spelling because of the vagaries of the Dutch registration system, which player did Bergkamp's dad name him after?

2. Arsenal paid £7.5 million for Bergkamp in 1995. Which Arsenal manager bought him, and which club sold him?

3. Bergkamp's first league goal for Arsenal came in a 4-2 win at Highbury on 23 September 1995, and ten days later, on the same ground, he scored his first cup goal in a 5-0 second-leg win in the League Cup. Arsenal's opponents on these two occasions came from opposite ends of the country. Who were they?

4. Dennis Bergkamp scored a sublime hat-trick in a 3-3 away draw in the Premier League on 27 August 1997. They were all great goals, but one of them was, as they say, different gravy! Which club conceded those three goals?

5. Which club from the fourth level of English football did Dennis Bergkamp score his 100th Arsenal goal against at Highbury on 4 January 2003 in the FA Cup third round?

6. Despite being arguably the classiest playmaker to have turned out for the club, Bergkamp could also dish it out when required, just ask the players who trained with him! He was no stranger to the odd red card, and the first one he received with Arsenal came from a high tackle in an away game at Sunderland in January 1997. The victim was one of the unluckiest players around because he played in four FA Cup finals and lost them all. Who was he?

7. What question can you ask about that amazing Bergkamp goal at Newcastle on 2 March 2002? Arsenal won 2-0. Who scored the unremembered goal?

8. With a perfect sense of timing, Bergkamp brought down the curtain on his Arsenal goalscoring with an 89th minute winner at Highbury on 15 April 2006, a day that had been designated 'Bergkamp Day'. Which club were condemned to play the bit-part role?

9. The very first game at The Emirates on 22 July 2006 was his testimonial. Who did Arsenal play?

10. How does the classical composer Richard Wagner figure in Dennis Bergkamp's career?

QUIZ No. 64

HIGHBURY HEROES – No.3 – HERBERT CHAPMAN

1. Which club was the only one Herbert Chapman played for and managed?

2. Which London club did Chapman play 50 times for between 1904 and 1907?

3. Which club that Herbert Chapman managed were expelled from the league after eight games of the 1919/20 season? When they came back, instead of the 'City' they left with they were now called 'United'.

4. Which club did Chapman's methods transform to such an extent that in the mid-1920s they became the first club to win three successive titles?

5. Upon taking over at Arsenal in 1925, Chapman revolutionised the club and set in place the structure that made them the team of the 1930s. In 1929 he made two key signings, one from Preston North End and the other from Exeter City, who both became Highbury legends. Who were they?

6. It took a while to turn the ship around in the league, although he did finish second in his first full season. The title finally came in the 1930/31 season when Arsenal broke the points record for the First Division with how many?

7. How many times under Chapman's management did Arsenal go to Wembley to contest an FA Cup Final?

8. A deep sadness pervaded the club when, after winning successive league titles, Chapman was on his way to a third when he died of pneumonia after scouting for players for the club against medical advice. Looking out for Arsenal's interests to the end, he died on 6 January of what year?

9. Which two players both topped the league goal charts for the Gunners three times under Chapman's reign?

10. The club commissioned a bust of Herbert Chapman that was situated in the entrance to Highbury's East Stand. When the move to The Emirates took place it was relocated there. Which highly respected sculptor undertook the commission?

QUIZ No. 65

HIGHBURY HEROES –
No.4 – TED DRAKE

1. Ted Drake started out playing for which club on the south coast?

2. Which Arsenal manager made what turned out to be a great decision in buying Ted Drake for £6,500 in March 1934 to solve the fact that Arsenal's former free scoring had dried up somewhat?

3. Drake made his league debut for the Gunners on 24 March 1934 against a Midlands club that turned out to be the team he scored more league goals against than any other. Who were they?

4. Drake's burst of scoring was very impressive and he scored 73 times in his first 77 games for the club. In 1934/35 he set a new Arsenal record for league goals in a season that hasn't been bettered and probably never will be. How many goals did he score?

5. Another Arsenal record that still stands is Drake's seven goals away from home on 14 December 1935 with just seven shots in the game. Who did Arsenal beat 7-1 that day on their own patch?

6. On which London ground that's still going strong did Ted Drake score four of the goals that gave Arsenal a 5-2 away win on 24 November 1934?

7. On which Lancastrian ground no longer going strong did Ted Drake grab another four-timer when Arsenal won 5-1 on New Year's Day 1937?

8. The war cut short Ted's career and he had to retire with a serious back injury sustained playing war-time football. It happened on the ground of the club he managed between 1947 and 1952. Who were they?

9. Which club did Ted Drake go on to manage to the league title in 1954/55 for the first time in their history in their Golden Jubilee Year?

10. In playing in and managing a title-winning side, Ted Drake was the first member of a small club. Which two men with Arsenal connections eventually joined him?

QUIZ No. 66

HIGHBURY HEROES – No.5 – GEORGE GRAHAM

1. George Graham was 17 when he came down from Scotland to join a Midlands club. Which one?

2. After signing for Arsenal in 1966, Graham played over 300 times for them in all competitions before joining Manchester United in 1972. How many times was he Arsenal's leading league scorer?

3. Why might George have mixed feelings about Wrexham's Racecourse Ground?

4. Which two London clubs besides Arsenal did George Graham play for?

5. In the first game of the 1970/71 season Arsenal drew 2-2 at Everton and George Graham got their second goal, but if you look at the scorers in the newspaper it appears that they have put his full name there instead of just his surname. Why?

6. As a manager he became noticed when he gained promotion from Division Three in 1984/85 with an unbeaten home record with which club?

7. 'If ever there was a player I felt definitely would not have what it took to be a manager it was George Graham. Running a nightclub? Yes. A football club? Absolutely not!' Which Arsenal manager got it wrong?

8. After George's unfortunate end to his great career in management at Arsenal in which he became the first man to land the club league titles in two different decades, he took the manager's position with which club in 1996?

9. In 1998 George Graham took over at White Hart Lane. Which two Arsenal players had previously managed there?

10. Some Arsenal fans might have thought that George's legacy was tarnished somewhat by his move across North London, but Spurs fans also didn't quite know what to make of it and ended up producing an eight-word grudging salute to him. What was it?

QUIZ No. 67

HIGHBURY HEROES – No.6 – THIERRY HENRY

1. From which club did Arsenal sign Thierry Henry in 1999?

2. Which is the only club that Thierry Henry has both played for and managed?

3. When he joined Arsenal he broke the record for the fastest 50 Premier League goals. How many matches did it take him?

4. Which tournament did he win the most times, the Copa del Rey with Barcelona or the FA Cup with Arsenal?

5. Which two North American clubs did he play for?

6. Who is the only non-English player with more Premier League goals to his name than Thierry Henry?

7. After such a distinguished career with Arsenal that it led to him winning a poll for the club's greatest-ever player, Thierry Henry returned on loan in January 2012 and immediately scored the winner at home in a third-round FA Cup tie, and in his final game for the club he got a last-minute winner. Arsenal's opponents in these two matches once fought out a memorable FA Cup Final nearly 50 years ago. Who were they?

8. Besides setting the goalscoring record for the French national side, Henry has also worked as an assistant coach for another nation in a World Cup. Which one?

9. It probably wasn't Thierry's greatest career moment when his unseen handball set up the goal that allowed France to qualify for the World Cup tournament at the expense of the Republic of Ireland in Paris on 18 November 2009, causing an almighty media storm into the bargain. Which other Arsenal player actually scored the goal that all the fuss was about?

10. During his days as a TV pundit for Sky Sports, in an incident that's been shown several times since, Thierry grabbed fellow pundit Jamie Carragher's thigh when what piece of football news was announced in the studio?

QUIZ No. 68

HIGHBURY HEROES –
No.7 – FRANK MCLINTOCK

1. From which club did Arsenal sign Frank McLintock in 1964?

2. Did McLintock play in more FA Cup finals for that club or for Arsenal?

3. McLintock's first Arsenal goal came in a 3-2 Boxing Day victory over which club in 1964 at Highbury?

4. A Denis Law hat-trick wasn't enough to save Scotland on the day Frank won his first cap for his country on 4 June 1963. They lost 4-3 to which Scandinavian country?

5. Ten days later, Scotland pulled off a spectacular victory when they won away by 6-2. It proved to be the occasion of McLintock's only goal for his country in a game that Scots can only dream about in today's sorry times. Who were their European opponents?

6. Frank McLintock scored twice for Arsenal just once. It was on 28 September 1966 when a side from the third flight of English football had taken Arsenal to a third match to decide a second-round League Cup tie. Having won the toss for home advantage, Arsenal duly obliged 5-0. Which club did they beat?

7. His only FA Cup goal for Arsenal came on 24 February 1973 in a 2-1 fifth-round win on a northern ground. He also scored just once for Arsenal in Europe in the Fairs Cup on 9 March 1971 in a 2-1 home win in the first leg of the quarter-final against a German club. The two clubs begin with the same letter. Who are they?

8. Which Midlands club did McLintock score more times against than any other club?

9. With which London club did McLintock end his career by playing for them 127 times in the League between 1973 and 1976?

10. Did Frank McLintock top 400 appearances in all competitions for Arsenal. Yes or no?

QUIZ No. 69

HIGHBURY HEROES – No.8 – JOE MERCER

1. In November 1946 which club, foolishly as it turned out, allowed the 32-year-old Joe Mercer to move south to Arsenal after he won the last league title with them before World War Two intervened?

2. It was a very shrewd move on the part of Arsenal manager George Allison because, although Joe's knees weren't great and any pace he had was gone, he was an inspirational figure and Arsenal played him in a more defensive role, very similar to Dave Mackay's move from Spurs to Derby County over 20 years later that led to promotion and the league title. How much did Arsenal pay for his services?
   (a) £7,000   (b) £10,000   (c) £13,000   (d) £16,000

3. Mercer played the first of 273 games for the Gunners on 30 November 1946 in a 2-2 draw at Highbury against which Lancastrian opponents?

4. Mercer scored just three times in 417 league games for his two clubs. His two for Arsenal came within a month of each other in February and March of 1953. They were scored against two clubs from Lancashire who each had a player that fans flocked in their thousands to see just after the war. Who were the two teams?

5. Mercer led Arsenal to two league titles and an FA Cup win and holds a record that links his playing days with his management experience, a record that is unique to English football. What is it?

6. Which team was Mercer caretaker manager of in 1974?

7. After Arsenal had won the league in 1953, Mercer announced his retirement with his 39th birthday looming, only to change his mind, and, come August, he led the Gunners out again for another season. Sadly, on 10 April 1954 he broke his leg at Highbury, saluting the crowd for the last time as he was stretchered off. Who were Arsenal playing that day?

8. As a manager Mercer had spells at Sheffield United, Coventry City and Aston Villa, before enjoying enormous success at Manchester City in the late 1960s and early 1970s. Which trophy did he win at both Aston Villa and Manchester City?

9. Mercer shares his name with someone who was famous in another sport at broadly the same time. Which sport?

10. This very special football man died on 9 August 1990. What fact added poignancy to Mercer's death?

QUIZ No. 70

HIGHBURY HEROES – No.9 – DAVID SEAMAN

1. David Seaman started out with one club that he never got to play for, making his debut with another club. Which two clubs were involved here?

2. David Seaman played in more than 50 European games for Arsenal. True or false?

3. David Seaman joined Arsenal from Queens Park Rangers in 1990 for £1.3 million and made his debut on 25 August, keeping a clean sheet away to another London club in a 3-0 win on the season's opening day. Which team did Arsenal beat that day?

4. When you think of David Seaman you think of that save in the FA Cup semi-final at Old Trafford on 13 April 2003. Incredible stuff! Who did they beat 1-0 that day with his miraculous intervention and which player was denied the goal he must have thought was his?

5. David Seaman made his England debut in a 1-1 draw on 16 November 1988 in a climate somewhat warmer than ours. Who did England play?

6. It was a game dominated by Arsenal players. Tony Adams scored England's goal, David Rocastle was earning his second cap while no fewer than three other Arsenal players were making their England debuts alongside David Seaman, two midfielders and a centre-forward. Who were the three?

7. Outside of Arsenal, which two clubs that David Seaman played for in his career have met each other in an FA Cup Final?

8. David Seaman finished his international career with 75 England caps. Which other goalkeeper has been capped 75 times for England?

9. David Seaman played in five FA Cup finals for Arsenal. Who was the only player to score twice against him in any of them?

10. How many games did David Seaman play for Arsenal in all competitions?
    (a) 360 (b) 460 (c) 560 (d) 660

QUIZ No. 71

HIGHBURY HEROES –
No.10 – PATRICK VIEIRA

1. With which French club did Patrick Vieira begin his football career in 1994?

2. Which is the only city that Patrick Vieira has played in for more than one club?

3. Did Patrick Vieira play more or less than 100 times for France?

4. In the FA Cup, League Cup and European competition, Patrick Vieira appeared 127 times for Arsenal, scoring just five goals. In which of the three contexts did he fail to score?

5. Vieira's first Arsenal appearance, as a substitute, came on 16 September 1996 in a home game against a side from Yorkshire. His first goal for the club arrived at Highbury on 7 December of the same year against a club not from Yorkshire, but geographically close to the other club. Who were the two clubs?

6. Vieira scored against Spurs in both the Premier League and the FA Cup. True or false?

7. Patrick was no stranger to a battle, as his epic duels with Roy Keane clearly demonstrated, but at the start of the 2000/01 season he managed to get sent off in both of Arsenal's opening two league games within 48 hours of each other. Who were the two opponents?

8. What was the occasion of Vieira's very last kick of the ball in a competitive context in an Arsenal shirt?

9. Which club did Vieira play for against Arsenal at Highbury in the Champions League on 28 March 2006?

10. Which two clubs beginning with the same letter has Patrick Vieira managed?

QUIZ No. 72

HIGHBURY HEROES –
No.11 – ARSENE WENGER

1. Arsene Wenger's first match as Arsenal's manager in October 1996 and his last match in that capacity in May 2018 were against the two teams that contested the 1928 FA Cup Final. Who were they?

2. Wenger has managed two clubs that begin with the letter 'N'. Who are they?

3. When Wenger managed Monaco which two ex-Spurs stars played for him?

4. Which trophy did Arsene Wenger win more times than anyone else in the game's history while managing Arsenal, and how many times did he win it?

5. Which player did Wenger buy in 1997 and sell in 1999 for 47 times what he paid for him?

6. Early on in his Arsenal managerial career the players had a nickname for Wenger based on a character in a film. What was it?

7. In October 2009 Wenger became the longest serving manager in the history of the club. Which previous Arsenal manager's record did he break?

8. Which Arsenal player is quoted here concerning Arsene's arrival at Highbury: 'At first I thought what does this Frenchman know about football, he wears glasses and looks more like a schoolteacher. Does he even speak English properly?'

9. A lot of players scored goals for Arsenal during Wenger's tenure of 22 years, but who were the two players who scored his first and last Arsenal goals?

10. The celebrations and standing ovations came for Wenger in his last home game in charge on 6 May 2018 when he signed off with a 5-0 win. Who were they playing?

QUIZ No. 73

HIGHBURY HEROES – No.12 – IAN WRIGHT

1. From which club did Arsenal sign Ian Wright in 1991?

2. Having scored in the FA Cup Final for that club in 1990, Wright then scored for Arsenal in the 1993 FA Cup Final. Who is the only other post-war Arsenal player to score for Arsenal and another club in an FA Cup Final?

3. In which competition did Ian Wright score 29 goals in 29 games for Arsenal?

4. Which is the only league club that both Ian Wright and Paul Gascoigne have played for?

5. Ian Wright's international career began on 6 February 1991 at Wembley against which African nation?

6. Wright's first goal for England was a vital one, and came on 29 May 1993 in an away World Cup qualifier. His goal made it 1-1 in the 84th minute against which country?

7. On 13 September 1997 Ian Wright scored a Highbury hat-trick that sent him to the top of the Arsenal goalscorers chart. Who was the game against and whose record did he break?

8. Ian Wright scored four times in a game just once, in a 4-2 home league win at Highbury on 21 December 1991. An early Christmas present for the fans. Who were Arsenal's opponents that day?

9. During his career Wright played a handful of games for two clubs who have been winners of the European Cup. Who are they?

10. Wright scored two hat-tricks against Ipswich Town during his time at Arsenal, but another club would have been happier still when he announced his retirement because not only did he score his first Arsenal hat-trick against them, but he went on to get three hat-tricks at their expense, two of which were on their own soil. Who were they?

QUIZ No. 74

THE 100 CLUB

Here is a list of 24 Arsenal goalscorers, the majority of them being members of the 100 club, having scored 100 or more goals for Arsenal in all competitions. The least number any of them have scored for the club is 77. Study them and consider the questions below.

JOE BAKER – CLIFF BASTIN – DENNIS BERGKAMP
JIMMY BRAIN – TED DRAKE – GEORGE GRAHAM
THIERRY HENRY – DAVID HERD – CLIFF HOLTON
JOE HULME – DAVID JACK – JACK LAMBERT – REG LEWIS
DOUG LISHMAN – PAUL MERSON – ROBERT PIRES
JOHN RADFORD – DON ROPER – ALAN SMITH
FRANK STAPLETON – GEOFF STRONG
ALAN SUNDERLAND – ROBIN VAN PERSIE – IAN WRIGHT

1. Who was the first of them to score 100 Arsenal goals?

2. Which two of them are the only ones to score over 100 goals over three different decades?

3. Who is the only player on the list to miss joining the 100 club by one goal, finishing his Arsenal career on 99?

4. Which player's haul was exactly 100 goals, all of them coming in the 1960s?

5. Four on the list all left Arsenal to join the same club. Who are the four players and which club did they join?

6. Which player on the list played the most games for Arsenal?

7. Who are the only two players on the list to score for Arsenal in the same FA Cup Final?

8. Can you list the top four Arsenal scorers on the list in the correct order?

9. Who was the first man to score 100 Arsenal goals at Highbury?

10. Who scored his goals at the fastest rate?

QUIZ No. 75

INTERNATIONALS - ENGLAND (POST-WAR)

1. Two Arsenal players with names beginning with the letter 'J' have each played just once for England. Who are they?

2. Which Arsenal player holds the post-war record for the oldest England debutant when he played in England's 4-2 win over Wales at Sunderland's Roker Park on 15 November 1950 at the age of 38?

3. Which two Arsenal centre-halves whose names begin with the letter 'B' gained three England post-war caps between them?

4. Who is the only player capped while at Arsenal to reach over 100 England caps in his overall career?

5. Which two post-war Arsenal forwards were capped at Arsenal and also while with a non-English club? The two clubs involved were Hibernian and Cologne.

6. Which three Arsenal players have been capped for England while at the club in both the 20th and 21st centuries?

7. Which player is the only man to represent England while at three Italian clubs? His caps while at Arsenal came in the 1990s.

8. Which two surnames have appeared twice among post-war Arsenal internationals for England?

9. Which two players have been capped post-war for England while with both Arsenal and Everton?

10. The two full-backs in that famous Arsenal defence, Lee Dixon and Nigel Winterburn, won all their England caps in the 1990s. Lee's total was 11 times that of Nigel's. How many caps did each of them win?

QUIZ No. 76

INTERNATIONALS - SCOTLAND & WALES (POST-WAR)

1. This Arsenal centre-half ended up one short of 100 outings for the Gunners in all competitions between 1948 and 1953 and received 21 Welsh caps. Apparently he was always apprehensive about playing away to Millwall! Who was he?

2. Tough guy defender never short of an opinion who joined Arsenal from Preston North End in 1958, playing 90 times in all competitions for the Gunners and winning 25 Scottish caps before becoming a manager of many clubs. Who was he?

3. Most Arsenal fans were sorry to see a player of his quality be allowed to go abroad in 2019, by which time he had played 58 times for Wales. Who was he?

4. Clever, creative inside-forward who won the FA Cup with Arsenal in 1950, and whose sole Scottish cap came against Northern Ireland at Hampden Park in 1952. Who was he?

5. In the 1950s he played 162 games in all competitions for Arsenal and represented Wales on 19 occasions, playing as a wing-half. Who was he?

6. Capped 11 times for Scotland, he played over 200 times for Arsenal in all competitions at centre-half between 1963 and 1969 before trying his luck at Old Trafford. Who was he?

7. The brother of a very famous footballer, he played up front for Arsenal on 64 occasions, scoring 28 goals, and gained 31 Welsh caps in a career that spanned the mid-1950s to the mid-1960s. Who was he?

8. Tough tackling wing-half at Arsenal between 1948 and 1956, playing 239 games for them in all competitions. He was capped 14 times for Scotland when with Arsenal and Sheffield United. Who was he?

9. Trouble seemed to follow this centre-forward around. He was capped for Wales while at Arsenal, and by the time he had finished he had been capped at four other clubs and had amassed 51 caps between 1995 and 2006. Who was he?

10. Versatile forward who played in 103 league fixtures for Arsenal and received seven caps for Scotland between 1953 and 1959. His career also took in Portsmouth, Wolves and Fulham. Who was he?

QUIZ No. 77

INTERNATIONALS – NORTHERN IRELAND AND THE REPUBLIC OF IRELAND (POST-WAR)

1. The League Cup may not have slipped through Tony Adams's hands, but this poor bloke did! During his time at Arsenal he played 85 games in all competitions in the 1990s and his career caps total for Northern Ireland was 39. Who was he?

2. Liam Brady needs no introduction and he was capped 72 times for the Republic of Ireland between 1975 and 1990, with Arsenal, four Italian clubs and one other English club. Which one?

3. Sammy Nelson played 338 times in all competitions for Arsenal and received 51 caps for his native Northern Ireland between 1970 and 1982, nearly all of them at Arsenal. At which other club was he capped for his country?

4. Niall Quinn started out at Arsenal and ended up with 92 caps for the Republic. Which two other clubs was he capped at?

5. This defender played in all three of Arsenal's FA Cup finals between 1978 and 1980 and gained 49 caps for Northern Ireland. Who was he?

6. This tricky left-winger played over 100 times for Arsenal between 1954 and 1961 before his transfer to Blackburn Rovers. He also turned out 32 times for the Republic. Who was he?

7. He received 59 Northern Ireland caps between 1961 and 1973 and was the only Arsenal man from that country to both play for and manage the club. Who was he?

8. This central-defender got 68 Republic of Ireland caps between 1977 and 1993, once scored a vital penalty for them in a World Cup shoot out and did get the odd game for Arsenal as well! Who was he?

9.   In the early 1960s this goalkeeper played 49 times for Arsenal in all competitions and got six caps for Northern Ireland. His Arsenal total would have been much higher but for the consistency of Jack Kelsey. Who was he?

10. Centre-forward Frank Stapleton was capped 71 times for the Republic of Ireland. His caps came at Arsenal, Manchester United, Derby County, Blackburn Rovers and two foreign clubs, one Dutch and the other French. Who were they?

INTERNATIONALS - OVERSEAS - PART 1

Here are ten Arsenal players. Which countries did they play for?

1. Philippe Senderos

2. Kolo Toure

3. Igors Stepanovs

4. Thomas Vermaelen

5. David Ospina

6. Henrikh Mkhitaryan

7. Mohamed Elneny

8. Sokratis

9. Lucas Torreira

10. Emmanuel Adebayor

INTERNATIONALS - OVERSEAS - PART 2

Here are another ten Arsenal players. Which countries did they play for?

1. Lauren

2. Alex Manninger

3. Andre Arshavin

4. Nicklas Bendtner

5. Emmanuel Frimpong

6. Santi Cazorla

7. Tomas Rosicky

8. Mathieu Flamini

9. Alexis Sanchez

10. Nwankwo Kanu

QUIZ No. 80

LEAGUE CUP FINALS

1. Arsenal reached the League Cup Final two years running in 1968 and 1969 but failed to get their hands on the trophy. Who scored their only goal in those defeats by Swindon Town and Leeds United?

2. Apparently, Liverpool had never lost a game in which Ian Rush scored for them, but that changed after he had given Liverpool the lead in the 1987 League Cup Final. Whose two strikes brought the League Cup to Highbury for the first time?

3. The winner in the 1987 League Cup Final had been neatly set up by someone who had come off the bench, but in the following year against Luton Town he was himself substituted for someone who came on and scored, although it was to no avail as Arsenal lost. Who are the two Arsenal players involved here?

4. 1993 produced a unique situation with the same two clubs, Arsenal and Sheffield Wednesday, contesting both domestic cup competitions. Which two players whose surnames begin with the same letter scored the goals that got them over the line in the League Cup Final that year?

5. What innovation concerning kit was seen for the first time at that 1993 League Cup Final at Wembley?

6. Arsenal lost 2-1 to Chelsea in the League Cup Final of 2007 at the Millennium Stadium in Cardiff in a match that boiled over at the end with three players being sent off. Who had given Arsenal a 12th-minute lead before all the mayhem?

7. 2011 saw the really big kick in the teeth where Arsenal fans were concerned when Arsenal managed to engineer a defensive calamity that ended up with the trophy in Birmingham instead of London. Who had earlier found the net for Arsenal with a first-half volley?

8. Which three players have scored twice against Arsenal in a League Cup Final? It happened in 1969, 1988 and 2007.

9. Which three clubs have scored three times against Arsenal in a League Cup Final?

10. Whose missed penalty in the 1988 League Cup Final that would have put the Gunners two ahead with not long to go proved costly in the end?

QUIZ No. 81

MAD MATCHES

1. On 3 November 1962 Blackburn Rovers and Arsenal met in a league match at Ewood Park that was hailed by the press as 'a ten-goal thriller.' How did the game end up?

2. There were another ten goals when Arsenal visited Bramall Lane to play Sheffield United on 7 January 1928. How did this one resolve itself?

3. In that same year of 1928 Arsenal met Liverpool at Highbury twice in separate seasons on 7 March and 27 October. They won the first game and drew the second. How many goals did the two games produce?

4. Arsenal were involved in the only top-flight league game to end in a 6-6 draw. It happened away to a Midlands club on 21 April 1930. Who were the hosts on this unique occasion?

5. Which two clubs have Arsenal beaten 7-3, one at Highbury in 1956 and the other at The Emirates in 2012? If you need a clue, they played each other in an FA Cup Final in the 1950s.

6. By what score did Arsenal beat Chelsea in 1958, Manchester City in 1961 and Wolves in 1962, all at Highbury?

7. A once-famous club no longer playing in the Football League beat Arsenal 7-4 on 7 November 1896. Who were they?

8. Many people know that Arsenal lost 5-4 to Manchester United at Highbury in 1958, five days before the Munich air crash, but, just over four years later, Arsenal lost by the same score on the same ground to the team that had played Manchester United in the FA Cup Final before Munich. Who were they?

9. Arsenal went out of the League Cup on penalties at Anfield in the 2019/20 season, but not before a truly stirring encounter. What was the score?

10. I've left the craziest one to last. In the League Cup fourth round on 30 October 2012 Arsenal travelled to Reading and found themselves 4-0 down after 37 minutes. After a great fight back that saw a daft incident when Arsenal players gave their shirts to fans before the game was over, and a Theo Walcott hat-trick into the bargain, they eventually went through after extra time. By what score?

QUIZ No. 82

MANAGERS

1. Who is the only Arsenal manager to win the League Cup?

2. Which Arsenal manager from 1904–08 doubles as a racecourse on the Scottish borders?

3. Who was managing the club the first time they won the FA Cup in 1930?

4. Who was in charge when Arsenal did the double in 1970/71?

5. Which two post-war Arsenal managers played for Everton?

6. Who is the only post-war Arsenal manager to have been a goalkeeper in his career as a player?

7. Who is the only post-war Arsenal manager to have won the 'Footballer of the Year' award as a player?

8. Which three post-war Arsenal players, with nearly 500 appearances for the club between them, have all managed West Bromwich Albion?

9. He was one of the most loved and respected figures in Arsenal's history, playing for them after World War One, becoming their trainer in the inter-war period, and successfully managing them from 1947 until his death in 1956. Who was he?

10. Arsenal have had, not counting caretakers, 13 post-war managers. Have more or less than half of them been ex-Arsenal players?

QUIZ No. 83

MULTIPLE CHOICE

1.   Who are the only club Arsenal have lost to in both an FA Cup Final and a League Cup Final?
(a) Chelsea (b) Leeds United (c) Liverpool (d) Manchester City

2.   Which side did Arsenal score six times in 18 minutes against in a 7-1 win at Highbury on 15 February 1992?
(a) Norwich City (b) Blackburn Rovers (c) QPR
(d) Sheffield Wednesday

3.   Arsenal have won the League title 13 times. Nine clubs have finished as runners-up to them. Only one of them have been runners-up to them on three occasions. Who are they?
(a) Liverpool (b) Aston Villa (c) Manchester United
(d) Huddersfield Town

4.   Who is the only Arsenal player to be sent off against Spurs at the old Wembley?
(a) Martin Keown (b) Ray Parlour (c) Lee Dixon
(d) Tony Adams

5.   Who are the only club to have beaten Arsenal in more than one FA Cup Final?
(a) Leeds United (b) West Ham United (c) Newcastle United
(d) Liverpool

6.   Between 1930/31 and 1934/35 Arsenal won four of a possible five league titles. By winning it in 1931/32, which club stopped Arsenal winning it five times in a row?
(a) Everton (b) Sheffield Wednesday (c) Manchester City
(d) Sunderland

7.   Which one of these Arsenal managers did not win the FA Cup?
(a) George Allison (b) George Swindin (c) Tom Whittaker
(d) Terry Neill

8. When Arsenal won the league in 2001/02 and 2003/04 they were undefeated away from home in both seasons. Who are the only team besides Arsenal to have gone through a season undefeated away from home?
(a) Preston North End (b) Liverpool (c) Aston Villa
(d) Manchester United

9. In which city have Arsenal played in two European finals?
(a) Paris (b) Brussels (c) London (d) Copenhagen

10. Arsenal have beaten both clubs from which city in an FA Cup Final at Wembley?
(a) Birmingham (b) Sheffield (c) Manchester (d) Liverpool

QUIZ No. 84

OPENING DAYS

1. In the 1990s Arsenal had a home game on the first day a significant number of seasons in a row. It looked unlikely it would be surpassed, but in this century it has been. How many times in a row have Arsenal experienced a home fixture to start the season in this century?

2. Arsenal lost 3-2 to Liverpool at Anfield on 22 August 1964 in the season's first game. What was significant about that match?

3. Arsenal and Spurs have met twice on the opening day of a season. In 1925 Spurs won 1-0 at Highbury, while, in 1968, Arsenal won 2-1 at White Hart Lane. One of Arsenal's goals that day was an own goal. Who scored the other one?

4. On 15 August 1992 Arsenal were unsurprisingly at home on the opening day. Lee Dixon had the ball wide on the right near the halfway line and was looking to clip the ball forward into space. Finding nothing on, he turned and chipped a long ball back to his goalkeeper. The problem was that he caught the ball with slightly more force than he intended and it sailed over the keeper's head and into his own net. You couldn't help but admire it! Arsenal never recovered, losing 4-2 to which club?

5. Arsenal have made two post-war visits to the seaside to start a season, with mixed results. They lost 3-1 up north in 1955 and won 4-0 down south in 1979. Which two clubs did they play?

6. Which northern ground have Arsenal opened the season on the most times?

7. Which London club, in the only season in their history that they spent in the top flight, hosted Arsenal on 18 August 1962 for their first game at that level, going down 2-1?

8. Which club that is no longer in the league beat Arsenal 5-1 in the first game of the 1927/28 season?

9. Who scored a hat-trick when Arsenal got off to a great start by winning 4-1 at Everton on 28 August 1937?

10. Which London club did Arsenal beat 5-1 away on the opening day of the 1988/89 season in a game in which Alan Smith got a hat-trick?

QUIZ No. 85

OUTGUNNED BY PEASHOOTERS! (GIANT KILLING)

This is a section that won't bring back pleasant memories for Arsenal fans, especially those a bit long in the tooth. Have a stiff drink and go for it!

1. Widely touted as the greatest of all cup upsets, it took place in the Midlands on 14 January 1933 in the FA Cup third round when the mighty Arsenal went down 2-0 to which club from the third level of English football?

2. The 1950s produced a few FA Cup problems for the Gunners, the first of which came on their own ground in the fourth round on 30 January 1954 when which Third Division South club beat them 2-1?

3. On 7 January 1956 Arsenal just managed to avoid the biggest shock of all when they were held to a 2-2 draw at Highbury in the FA Cup third round. This time, though, it was a non-league club, and 15,000 wedged themselves into their ground for the replay where Arsenal edged them out 2-1. Who were they?

4. Arsenal were becoming vulnerable to this sort of thing, and on 4 January 1958 they were knocked out of the FA Cup again in the third round by 3-1 to a Division Three South side with an inappropriate name for that division. Who were they?

5. In the 1960s a very progressive club not long in the league who had a reputation for giant killing took aim at Arsenal in the FA Cup fourth round on 30 January 1965. They hit the target too, beating them 2-1. Who were they?

6. Arsenal's unfortunate experience in the 1969 League Cup Final has been dealt with elsewhere, but which Third Division club from the North West beat them 1-0 in that same competition in the 1973/74 season?

7. In the FA Cup in 1984/85 Arsenal nearly came unstuck at Hereford in the third round but won the replay 7-2. However, more problems came their way in Yorkshire in the next round when they lost to a Division Three club through a last-minute penalty. Who beat them?

8. The penalty taker partially redeemed himself to Arsenal fans by scoring against Spurs when playing for Coventry City in the 1987 FA Cup Final. Who was he?

9. Arsenal, as league champions, must have gone with some confidence to this Division Four club for an FA Cup third-round tie in 1991/92. They didn't return with any after going down 2-1 to which club?

10. New century, same banana skins! Which Yorkshire club from three flights below beat Arsenal on penalties in the League Cup quarter-final in 2013?

QUIZ No. 86

PENALTIES

1. Bobby Buist was Arsenal's first scorer from the spot on Boxing Day 1893 when Woolwich Arsenal lost 3-1 at Grimsby. But the man who scored the most penalties for Arsenal in that century was someone who shared his surname with a member of England's legendary 1966 team. Who was he? Have a go, it's a 10-1 shot and they do come in sometimes!

2. The only two clubs Arsenal beat in a penalty shoot-out in the FA Cup in the 20th century both lost to them in their 'double' year of 1997/98, one in the third round and the other in the sixth. Which two clubs had their Wembley dreams shattered?

3. When the new century arrived we were only 19 days into it when Arsenal were on the receiving end, going out of the FA Cup in the fourth round 6-5 in a penalty shoot-out after two 0-0 draws failed to produce an outcome against which Midlands club?

4. Arsenal's first goal from the penalty spot in the FA Cup came in a 1-1 home draw with West Ham United on 13 January 1906. The goalscorer shares his surname with two Everton players who have both scored in FA Cup finals, one in the very next season and the other in 1984. Who was the goalscorer?

5. Arsenal's first goal from the spot in Europe came on 4 November 1970 in a 2-0 home win over Sturm Graz. Who took it?

6. Who scored Arsenal's first post-war penalty in the league on 16 November 1946 in a 4-2 win at Highbury, and who did they beat? Here's a nice clue. He worked alongside Inspector Morse, and all detectives need these to solve cases. Got it?

7. On 22 October 2005 two Arsenal players made a ridiculous mess of a penalty in a league game at Highbury that they actually won with another penalty. Who were the culprits who were being too clever by half, and who were the bemused visitors?

8.   Arsenal's first post-war FA Cup goal from the penalty spot came in a 2-1 home win over Swansea Town in the fourth round on 28 January 1950, a year in which the Gunners went on to win it. The scorer is an area of south-west London. Who was he?

9.   Arsenal won through to the next round in domestic cup competitions three years running on penalties in 2003/04, 2004/05 and 2005/06. The middle one was in the FA Cup and the others were in the League Cup. The shoot-outs were won 9-8, 4-2 and 3-1 against three Yorkshire clubs. Who were they?

10. On the way to the 1995 European Cup Winners' Cup Final, Arsenal drew their semi-final 5-5 on aggregate against Sampdoria. David Seaman was the hero of the subsequent 3-2 penalty shoot-out win. He was beaten by someone who went on to win the Premier League as a manager and saved the kick of someone who later played for Crystal Palace. Who were the two players?

QUIZ No. 87

QUOTES

1. 'Arsenal caress a football the way I dreamed of caressing Marilyn Monroe.' Which legendary manager pays tribute to Wenger's team in a way that someone would surely complain about in today's world?

2. 'When he stops playing football, he can go into acting.' Arsenal defender Lauren suggests there's a Hollywood career for which Manchester United player?

3. 'For Tony to admit he was an alcoholic took an awful lot of bottle.' Which Arsenal team-mate produced unintended amusement here?

4. 'If he thinks he's going to set the world alight he can forget it. When the fog, ice and cold arrive he won't want to know.' Which football club chairman's comments on Dennis Bergkamp's move to Arsenal made him look rather stupid in hindsight?

5. 'When Wimbledon hit long balls up to a 6ft 2in black centre-forward it's destroying the game. When Arsenal hit long balls to a 6ft 4in Irishman it's good football.' Which manager was feeling hard done by in 1989?

6. 'Anyone who didn't enjoy Arsenal tonight, even if they are a Norwich supporter, should start looking at another sport.' Which Norwich City manager is magnanimous after his team have been beaten 4-1 at home by Arsenal in the 2004/05 season?

7. 'House prices in London are a nightmare. I have a nice home between Sheffield and Barnsley, but a £50,000 property up there is £200,000 down here.' Which player is talking about his move from Sheffield Wednesday to Arsenal in 1988?

8. 'There were only three tackles on him, that hardly constitutes the Texas Chainsaw Massacre.' Alex Ferguson plays down his team's physicality in ending Arsenal's 49-game unbeaten run. Which Arsenal player was he talking about?

9. 'At least we got a point.' Which Arsenal player forgets it's not a league game while playing for England in a 1-1 draw against Portugal in a Wembley friendly?

10. 'The sending off is big ammunition for people like me who think that one little screen in front of the fourth official is a big help against this kind of mistake.' Which manager is talking about Andre Marriner's error in showing a red card to Gibbs instead of Oxlade-Chamberlain? Of course, when they finally got that little screen they declined to use it. Instead they spent fortunes setting up a bunker 100 miles away where people were paid to suck the spirit out of the game.

QUIZ No. 88

RECKLESS REDS

1. Which two Arsenal players were sent off in the 2007 League Cup Final against Chelsea?

2. Who is the only player to be sent off for England while a player at Arsenal? It happened away to Poland in 1973.

3. Which Arsenal player, who also played for two other clubs, was sent off 13 times in his career, putting him in a very creditable third place in the all-time table?

4. Which Arsenal player has the Premier League record for red cards with a total of nine?

5. Which Arsenal player was sent off at Wembley in a Champions League game against Lens in 1998?

6. An Arsenal man holds the record for the quickest sending off in the League Cup, when he lasted just 33 seconds after coming on as a substitute against Birmingham City at Highbury on 14 October 1997. It's a difficult question because his Arsenal career consisted of three outings from the subs bench, but who was he?

7. Which Arsenal player in October 1988 was banned for nine matches for breaking the jaw of Southampton's Glenn Cockerill?

8. Which Arsenal goalkeeper was sent off on 1 October 2014 at The Emirates in a Champions League group stage game against Galatasaray?

9. Which Arsenal player received a red card playing for England under-21s against Croatia at Upton Park on 19 August 2003?

10. Which Arsenal man was unable to take part in the penalty shoot-out that decided the 2005 FA Cup Final in Arsenal's favour because he had become the second player to be sent off in an FA Cup Final?

QUIZ No. 89

SHARPSHOOTERS

All these players have been Arsenal's leading scorer in a season.

1. Who topped the Arsenal scoring charts three years running in 1929/30, 1930/31 and 1931/32?

2. Who was the only player to be leading scorer for Arsenal in both the 1980s and the 1990s?

3. Who was Arsenal's leading goalscorer for five successive seasons in the 1950s?

4. Thierry Henry holds the record for the number of successive seasons he topped the Arsenal scoring list. How many seasons was it?

5. Which three Arsenal players beginning with a 'W' have been their top goalscorer in a post-war season?

6. Going to the opposite end of the alphabet, which three Arsenal players with names beginning with an 'A' have been top goalscorer since the 1990s?

7. Which two Arsenal players, whose names begin with the same letter, both won the Arsenal top scorer accolade twice in the 1970s?

8. Who was Arsenal's leading goalscorer in the five seasons leading up to World War Two?

9. Who is the only Spaniard to top Arsenal's goalscoring charts?

10. From the sublime to the ridiculous! Charlie Randall was Arsenal's top scorer over their 38 league games of the 1912/13 season. Arsenal were relegated that year and his goals total is the lowest-ever number to be top scorer with. How many did he get?

QUIZ No. 90

TRANSFERS - 1946-59

1. Which inside-forward, who scored 68 goals in 132 games for Arsenal between 1953 and 1958, moved to Cardiff City in that year?

2. Which club supplied Arsenal in the 1950s with Stan Charlton, Vic Groves and Len Julians, who together played nearly 350 games for the Gunners?

3. Prolific scorer Don Roper came to Arsenal from this club in 1947 and ten years later, after 95 goals in 319 games, he went back to the club he came from. Who were they?

4. Archie Macaulay, Tommy Lawton and Jimmy Bloomfield all joined Arsenal from the same London club. Which one?

5. Which centre-half, who went on to play over 200 games for Arsenal, did they sign from Fulham in 1952?

6. He came from Walsall in 1948 and left for Nottingham Forest in 1956, but in those years he was at Arsenal he scored a handsome 135 goals for the club. Who was he?

7. Chances to perform for this tall centre-half were not in abundance because of the consistency of the answer to question five, but he still managed a total of 76 games for Arsenal before moving to Hearts after ten years at Highbury in 1959. Who was he?

8. One of Arsenal's best signings of the period, he came from Stockport County in 1954 and went on to score 107 goals for Arsenal. While at Stockport he enjoyed the rare feat of playing in a league game against Hartlepools with his father. Who was he?

9. Which tough-tackling player came from Preston North End in 1958 and left for Chelsea in 1961?

10. Late in 1946 he was in his mid-30s sitting in a bath after training with Fulham in Division Two when he was called to the phone. After asking who it was and being told it was Arsenal, he was sure it was a wind up. But it was Arsenal, and they thought he might be

the man to turn their chances into goals. They weren't far wrong, and by the time he moved on to Crystal Palace in 1949 he had contributed 68 goals in 88 league games. In 1947/48 he didn't miss a single league game and top scored with 33, helping the Gunners to the title. What a signing and what a story for a man as tough as they come. It only leaves you to tell me who he was?

QUIZ No. 91

TRANSFERS - 1960s

1. In the early 1960s Arsenal bought centre-half Ian Ure and winger Jimmy Macleod from which two Scottish clubs?

2. In 1960 Arsenal purchased an elegant inside-forward who had been locked in a dispute with his club for some time, and then, after over 200 games for the Gunners, they sold him. He came from black-and-white stripes and left for red-and-white stripes. Who was he, where did he come from and where did he go?

3. After giving excellent service to Arsenal, inside-left Jimmy Bloomfield and winger Alan Skirton both moved on, the former in 1960 and the latter six years later. The two clubs they joined begin with the same letter. Who were they?

4. Colin Addison came to Highbury in 1966 from Nottingham Forest as part of the deal that took which Arsenal player in the opposite direction?

5. Which Wolves player did Arsenal sign in 1961 to add a bit of bite to the midfield?

6. Which Newcastle born inside-forward, who had been on Arsenal's books since 1955, joined Nottingham Forest in 1964 after over 150 outings for the club?

7. In 1963 Arsenal bought a goalkeeper from Liverpool who went on to play for them in the 1968 League Cup Final against Leeds United. Who was he?

8. Which right-back, the son of a Fulham stalwart, played 46 games for Arsenal between 1960 and 1963 before joining Manchester City?

9. Which player did Arsenal buy from West Bromwich Albion in 1964, whose 74 games for the club were a very small part of his eventual value to Arsenal?

10. Which centre-forward did Coventry City sell to Arsenal in 1968?

QUIZ No. 92

TRANSFERS - 1970s

1. From which club did Arsenal sign Alan Sunderland in 1977?

2. The very well known Malcolm Macdonald came from Newcastle United in 1976. However, they also bought another player from that club in that same year. He was a centre-half who turned out just 19 times for the club before moving on to Birmingham City. Who was he?

3. Strangely enough, Arsenal bought not one but two central-defenders from Spurs in 1977. Who were they?

4. Which member of Arsenal's double-winning side of 1971 joined Wolves in 1975?

5. During the 1970s Arsenal's Alan Ball, Peter Marinello and Terry Neill all left to join clubs by the sea. Which three clubs were involved here?

6. Those two favourites Peter Storey and John Radford both moved on in the 1970s, the former in 1977 and the latter a year earlier. Which two London clubs did they go to?

7. A superb playmaker who had his best years at Chelsea, Alan Hudson came to Arsenal in 1976 and left in 1978. The club he came from and the club he went to both begin with the letter 'S'. Who were they?

8. Which player's Arsenal career was sandwiched between the two Manchester clubs, joining Arsenal from one of them in 1974 and leaving for the other in 1976?

9. After over 200 games in all competitions and a goal in an FA Cup Final for Arsenal, Eddie Kelly moved to another London club in 1976. Which one?

10. Three Arsenal men, Jon Sammels, George Armstrong and Jeff Blockley, all ended up at various points in the 1970s at the same club. Which one?

QUIZ No. 93

TRANSFERS - 1980s

1. Which midfielder who started exactly 150 games for Arsenal between 1981 and 1987 joined West Ham United in the latter year?

2. Arsenal players Brian McDermott and Tommy Caton both left the club in the 1980s, McDermott in 1984 and Caton in 1987. They both ended up at the same club. Which one?

3. Which two members of Arsenal's much-lauded defence came from Stoke City in 1988?

4. Paul Mariner came to the club from Ipswich Town in 1984, moving to a club with an appropriate name in 1986. Where did he go?

5. Which fiery midfielder came from Southampton in 1984 and made over 100 appearances in an Arsenal shirt before joining Luton Town in 1988?

6. In 1980, a man who had turned out over 500 times for Arsenal left the club to join Watford. Towards the end of the same decade, in 1987, another player whose name began with the same letter as the previous one made the journey in the opposite direction. Who were the two players?

7. Which member of that eventually famous defence joined Arsenal in 1987 from Wimbledon?

8. Which Italian club did legendary Arsenal player Liam Brady go to in 1980?

9. Midfielder Paul Nicholas came to Highbury in 1981, played 80 games in all competitions, and departed in 1983. The club he came from was also the club he went back to. Who were they?

10. Forwards Ian Allinson in 1983 and Perry Groves in 1986 both joined Arsenal from the same club. Which one?

QUIZ No. 94

TRANSFERS - 1990s

1. Centre-forward John Hartson and centre-half Matthew Upson both arrived at Highbury from the same club, Hartson in 1995 and Upson in 1997. Which club sold them to Arsenal?

2. Which two players came to the club from Monaco in 1997, both playing a part in the successful years that followed?

3. Which club did centre-forward Kevin Campbell join in 1995 after playing over 200 games and scoring 59 goals for Arsenal?

4. Stephen Morrow and Chris Kiwomya both left Arsenal in the late 1990s after struggling to hold a first-team place. They left to join the same London club. Which one?

5. Which striker, following the same route taken as Dennis Bergkamp four years earlier, joined Arsenal from Inter Milan in 1999?

6. Scorer of an FA Cup Final replay goal in 1993, central-defender Andy Linighan came to Highbury from Crystal Palace in 1990 and left to join which club in 1997 after playing over 150 times for Arsenal?

7. Which club did Arsenal strikers Ian Wright and John Hartson join in the late 1990s?

8. Leeds United signed two Arsenal players in the early 1990s. Firstly in 1990 they bought a goalkeeper who ended up with just short of 300 games for the Gunners and whose career looks like a table tennis match between the clubs! Secondly, in 1992 a very popular player with the fans went to Leeds United after 275 games in the Arsenal attack. Who were the two players?

9. Paul Merson played over 400 times for Arsenal in all competitions but moved on in 1997. Where to?

10. Andy Cole eventually made a great future for himself but appeared just once as a substitute during his time at Arsenal at the start of his career. After a loan spell at Fulham, which club did he join in 1992?

QUIZ No. 95

TRANSFERS - 2000s

1. Arsenal signed this French defender from one London club in 2006 and sold him to another London club in 2010. During his time at The Emirates he was very briefly club captain. Who was he?

2. Philippe Senderos, the central-defender, joined Arsenal in 2004. If you put the letter 'I' in the middle of the club he came from you get a table napkin. Who were they?

3. Which left-back did Monaco sell to Arsenal in 2005?

4. From which German outfit did Arsenal buy Tomas Rosicky in 2006?

5. Two Dutchmen signed for Arsenal during this period. Robin Van Persie arrived in 2004 and was followed by Thomas Vermaelen in 2009. Which two clubs sold them?

6. Gael Clichy came to the club in 2003 and became the youngest player to win the Premier League, while Sylvain Wiltord joined in 2000 for a new club-record fee of £13 million. Which two French clubs sold them?

7. Bacari Sagny in 2007 and Vassirki Diaby a year earlier came to Arsenal from the same French club. Which one?

8. Robert Pires in 2000, Mathieu Flamini in 2004 and Samir Nasri in 2008 all came to Arsenal from the same French club. Which one?

9. Which Dutchman arrived at Highbury from Glasgow Rangers in 2001?

10. Which Spanish club sold goalkeeper Vito Mannone to Arsenal in 2005?

QUIZ No. 96

TRANSFERS – 2010s

1. Hector Bellerin came to Arsenal from which club in 2011?

2. From which club did Calum Chambers come to Arsenal in 2014?

3. Which club sold Nacho Monreal to Arsenal in 2013?

4. From which French club, whose name invokes an English club, did Arsenal sign Matteo Guendouzi in 2018?

5. In this period, midfielder Mathieu Flamini returned to Arsenal after a spell in Italy. Which club did he rejoin Arsenal from?

6. Which classy, industrious midfielder came to Arsenal from Malaga in 2012?

7. French clubs Montpelier in 2012, and Olympique Lionnaise in 2017 sold two forwards to Arsenal. Who were they?

8. From which club did Arsenal buy defender Carl Jenkinson in 2011?

9. Pierre-Emerick Aubameyang came from Borussia Dortmund in 2018. Which other Arsenal player came from the same club in the same year?

10. Which defender joined Arsenal from German club Werder Bremen in 2011?

QUIZ No. 97

TRUE OR FALSE - PART 1

1. Arsenal were the lowest scorers in the Premier League's inaugural season of 1992/93. True or false?

2. Chelsea, Liverpool, Manchester United and Newcastle United have all played more than one FA Cup Final against Arsenal. True or false?

3. Arsenal are the only London club to lose in a Europa League Final since its inception in 2009/10. True or false?

4. Arsenal have won the Premier League three times, the first time with a points total in the 70s, the second time with a points total in the 80s, and finally, on the third time, with a total in the 90s. True or false?

5. Since the Premier League began, Arsenal are the only club to finish runners-up three times in a row. True or false?

6. The most decades in a row that Arsenal have won a league title in is three. True or false?

7. Arsenal have tasted defeat in seven FA Cup finals. On four of these occasions they lost by the only goal of the game. True or false?

8. Of the 14 clubs that Arsenal have faced in an FA Cup Final, only Hull City have never won the trophy. True or false?

9. Arsenal had a different goalkeeper in each of their FA Cup wins of 2014, 2015, 2017 and 2020. True or false?

10. Frank Stapleton scored more goals than Niall Quinn for the Republic of Ireland. True or false?

QUIZ No. 98

TRUE OR FALSE - PART 2

1. Chelsea are the only London club to play Arsenal in a League Cup Final. True or false?

2. David Seaman is the only man to play in goal for Arsenal in an FA Cup Final in two different decades. True or false?

3. The highest player on the England goalscorers list with an Arsenal connection is David Platt. True or false?

4. Arsenal have won the Premier League three times under Arsene Wenger, with a different club filling the runners-up spot on each occasion. True or false?

5. Arsenal have won the FA Cup more times in the first 20 years of this century than in all of the previous century. True or false?

6. Three players with Arsenal connections, Tommy Lawton, Tony Woodcock and Danny Welbeck, have all scored 16 goals in internationals for England. True or false?

7. Arsenal have been runners-up for the league title below five different clubs. They are Manchester United, Liverpool, Everton, Chelsea and Huddersfield Town. True or false?

8. Arsenal never won as many as 20 league games in a season throughout the 1960s. True or false?

9. Arsenal have never finished bottom of any league they have played in. True or false?

10. There have been more post-war Arsenal managers whose names begin with a 'W' than any other letter. True or false?

QUIZ No. 99

VENUES

1. Arsenal's first-ever FA Cup semi-final came in the 1905/06 season when they lost 2-0 to Newcastle United on a now defunct ground named for a monarch. What was it called?

2. Arsenal's first winning FA Cup semi-final came in the 1926/27 season when they beat Southampton 2-1 at a London venue that they have a two-out-of-two record on, having beaten Orient there 3-0 in 1977/78. What is the ground?

3. In 1971/72, after a 1-1 draw with Stoke City at Villa Park in the FA Cup semi-final, Arsenal went through 2-1 in the replay with shades of the previous year brought to mind. They won on Merseyside, but which of the possible two were hosts on this occasion?

4. Arsenal have played 12 semi-finals in the FA Cup on one particular ground, far exceeding all the others. Which ground is it?

5. Which is the only ground that Arsenal have played a semi-final on three years running, winning all three?

6. Which ground did Arsenal beat Blackburn Rovers 3-0 on in the FA Cup semi-final of 2004/05?

7. 1979/80 saw the only occasion that Arsenal had to play four matches before their semi-final could produce a winner. Their opponents were Liverpool and they drew 0-0 at Hillsborough and 1-1 twice at Villa Park before Arsenal squeezed through 1-0 in the fourth match at a now defunct Midlands ground. Which one was it?

8. Which is the only ground that Arsenal have won four FA Cup semi-finals on in just five trips there?

9. Which is the only city outside London that Arsenal have played in a semi-final on two if its grounds?

10. When Arsenal won through to the FA Cup Final in 1935/36 they beat Grimsby Town in the semi-final on a Yorkshire club's now defunct ground. What ground did they play on?

QUIZ No. 100

WHICH, WHAT, HOW, WHO AND WHY?

1. Who were the only club to twice be runners-up to Arsenal when they won their five league titles in the 1930s?

2. How are Shrewsbury, Charlton and Sunderland linked in Arsenal's history?

3. Which surname crops up the most among Arsenal players?
   (a) Shaw (b) Jones (c) Smith (d) Wilson

4. Who is missing from this list of Arsenal goalscorers in European finals? – Ray Kennedy, Eddie Kelly, John Radford, Jon Sammels, Alan Smith, Sol Campbell and Alex Iwobi?

5. Who are the only club that Arsenal have both won and lost an FA Cup semi-final against on the same ground?

6. Which club have Arsenal played in both an FA Cup Final and a League Cup Final without beating them in either?

7. Why is Arsenal's 7-1 win over Charlton Athletic in a Wembley cup final not in the record books?

8. What cigarette manufacturer is brought to mind when you join Arsenal's centre-forward in both their FA Cup finals of 1930 and 1932 with their centre-half in their first FA Cup Final in 1927 against Cardiff City?

9. Which Lancastrian club were the only team to have more points than Arsenal when the 1939/40 season was abandoned due to the outbreak of war after just three rounds of games?

10. To link the beginning of this marathon with the end, which London club were Arsenal playing in the scenes from a league game at Highbury in the film that was the answer to the third question in the very first quiz?

ANSWERS

QUIZ No. 1 ANYTHING GOES

1. 1960s
2. George Graham
3. The Arsenal Stadium Mystery
4. Manu Petit – France 1998
5. Robbie Lyle
6. Their surnames are all English kings
7. Senna
8. Gilberto Silva and Christian Zeige
9. Immobile and Aubameyang
10. It was the only instance of an Arsenal goalkeeper scoring

QUIZ No. 2 ARSENAL IN THE FOOTBALL LEAGUE 1893-1915

1. Newcastle United
2. Crewe
3. Loughborough Town
4. Preston North End
5. Eight
6. Charlie Satterthwaite
7. Blackburn Rovers
8. Sheffield Wednesday and Sunderland
9. Alf Common
10. They won three

QUIZ No. 3 ARSENAL IN THE FA CUP 1889-1915

1. Lyndhurst
2. Millwall
3. Newcastle United and Sheffield Wednesday
4. Gillingham
5. Ashford United
6. Brentford and Fulham
7. 6-0
8. Bristol
9. Merthyr Town (the guitarist was Mick Taylor)
10. Kingston Pavilion

QUIZ No. 4 ARSENAL IN THE FOOTBALL LEAGUE 1919-39

1. Henry Norris
2. D. Burgess, J. Butler, J. North, J. Rutherford, H. White, B. Blyth and A. Graham
3. Bradford City
4. Everton's Dixie Dean scored a hat-trick that took him to 60 goals for the season, a record that hasn't been beaten yet and never will be!
5. Jack Lambert and David Jack
6. Eight
7. Wolves
8. Seven
9. 13
10. 11

QUIZ No. 5 ARSENAL IN THE FA CUP 1919-39

1. Stamford Bridge
2. QPR and Chelsea
3. Preston North End
4. They were all original members of the Football League in 1888
5. Cardiff City
6. Hull City, Grimsby Town and Southampton
7. Crystal Palace
8. Darwen
9. Cliff Bastin
10. Ted Drake

QUIZ No. 6 ARSENAL IN THE FOOTBALL LEAGUE 1946-59

1. Wolves
2. Reg Lewis
3. Grimsby Town
4. They scored five goals in three successive home games
5. Stoke City
6. Spurs
7. Preston North End
8. Cliff Holton
9. Hearing a whistle in the crowd, he thought the referee had blown for full-time and slammed the ball into his own net to make it 4-1
10. David Herd

QUIZ No. 7 ARSENAL IN THE FA CUP 1945-59

1. West Ham United
2. White Hart Lane
3. They never played outside London
4. Reg Lewis
5. Chelsea
6. Norwich City and

Northampton Town
7. Freddie Cox
8. A printing strike had reduced the programme to a single folded sheet
9. Burnley and Aston Villa
10. Leyton Orient

QUIZ No. 8 ARSENAL IN THE FOOTBALL LEAGUE - THE 1960s

1. Six
2. Wolves
3. West Ham United
4. None – they didn't play on Boxing Day, but beat Birmingham City 4-1 away on the 28th
5. Sheffield
6. Geoff Strong and Alan Skirton
7. Five
8. John Radford
9. 4,500
10. Ten

QUIZ No. 9 ARSENAL IN CUP COMPETITIONS - THE 1960s

1. Liverpool
2. Birmingham City
3. Johnny MacLeod
4. West Bromwich Albion
5. John Radford
6. The fifth round
7. Gillingham
8. Tommy Baldwin
9. David Jenkins
10. Huddersfield Town

QUIZ No. 10 ARSENAL IN THE FOOTBALL LEAGUE - THE 1970s

1. George Armstrong, Frank McLintock and Bob Wilson
2. Stoke City
3. John Radford and Ray Kennedy
4. Nine
5. Peter Marinello
6. Won 14 Drew 14 Lost 14
7. Malcolm Macdonald
8. David O'Leary
9. Spurs, QPR and Chelsea
10. Pat Rice

QUIZ No. 11 ARSENAL IN CUP COMPETITIONS - THE 1970s

1. Stoke City
2. Alan Ball
3. Leicester City
4. Four
5. Brian Kidd
6. Malcolm Macdonald
7. Wolves, Walsall and Wrexham
8. Manchester
9. Nottingham
10. Sheffield Wednesday

QUIZ No. 12 ARSENAL IN THE FOOTBALL LEAGUE - THE 1980s

1. Kenny Sansom
2. Aston Villa – they had already won the league
3. John Hollins
4. April
5. Tony Woodcock
6. Viv Anderson
7. Nine
8. Portsmouth
9. John Lukic, David Rocastle and Nigel Winterburn
10. Brian Marwood

QUIZ No. 13 ARSENAL IN CUP COMPETITIONS - THE 1980s

1. Spurs
2. Manchester United
3. Walsall
4. Manchester City
5. Luton Town
6. Charlie Nicholas
7. Millwall
8. Alan Sunderland
9. Hereford United
10. Plymouth Argyle

QUIZ No. 14 ARSENAL IN THE LEAGUE - THE 1990s

1. Coventry City and Anders Limpar
2. 18 and Chelsea
3. QPR
4. No goals were scored either for or against
5. QPR again
6. Sampdoria and Inter Milan
7. Stewart Houston and Pat Rice

8. 18
9. Leeds United
10. Nwankwo Kanu

QUIZ No. 15 ARSENAL IN CUP COMPETITIONS - THE 1990s

1. Ian Wright
2. Spurs and Crystal Palace
3. Sheffield Wednesday
4. Hartlepool United
5. Millwall
6. Leeds United
7. Chelsea
8. Sheffield United
9. Dennis Bergkamp
10. (a) Coventry City (b) Crystal Palace (c) Scarborough (d) Yeovil Town (e) Barnsley (f) Cambridge United

QUIZ No. 16 ARSENAL IN EUROPE 1963-80

1. Copenhagen
2. 15,000
3. Ajax and Anderlecht
4. Cologne
5. Ajax
6. Red Star Belgrade
7. Valencia
8. Juventus
9. Paul Vaessen
10. John Radford

QUIZ No. 17 ARSENAL IN EUROPE - THE 1990s

1. Alan Smith
2. Paul Merson
3. Kevin Campbell
4. Parma
5. Real Zaragosa
6. Ian Wright
7. John Hartson
8. Wembley
9. Lens
10. Galatasaray

QUIZ No. 18 ARSENAL IN EUROPE - THE 2000s

1. Valencia
2. Thierry Henry
3. Inter Milan
4. Chelsea
5. Bayern Munich
6. Two
7. Sol Campbell
8. PSV
9. Slavia Prague and Liverpool
10. Roma

QUIZ No. 19 ARSENAL IN EUROPE - THE 2010s

1. Olivier Giroud and Laurent Koscielny
2. Danny Welbeck
3. Anderlecht
4. Monaco
5. 5-1
6. Diego Costa
7. Alex Oxlade-Chamberlain
8. Ainsley Maitland-Niles
9. Azerbaijan
10. Bayern Munich

QUIZ No. 20 ARSENAL - SEASON 2000/01

1. Manu Petit and Marc Overmars
2. Charlton Athletic
3. West Ham United
4. Middlesbrough
5. Manchester United and Leicester City
6. Ray Parlour
7. Sylvain Wiltord
8. QPR
9. Spurs and Chelsea
10. Ipswich Town

QUIZ No. 21 ARSENAL - SEASON 2001/02

1. December
2. Sylvain Wiltord
3. Leeds United
4. Charlton Athletic
5. Freddie Ljungberg
6. Lauren
7. Sol Campbell
8. Blackburn Rovers
9. Thierry Henry
10. Franny Jeffers

QUIZ No. 22 ARSENAL – SEASON 2002/03

1. Spurs and Newcastle United
2. Thierry Henry
3. Blackburn Rovers
4. Kolo Toure
5. Pascal Cygan
6. Robert Pires and Jermaine Pennant
7. Farnborough Town
8. Chelsea
9. Franny Jeffers
10. Lauren, Ljungberg and Luzhny

QUIZ No. 23 ARSENAL – SEASON 2003/04

1. They conceded 14 at home and 12 away
2. Portsmouth
3. Leeds United
4. Jens Lehmann
5. Jose Antonio Reyes
6. Middlesbrough
7. Jeremie Aliadiere
8. The first answer is that it was Arsenal's 50th red card under Arsene Wenger; while the second answer is Nicolas Anelka
9. Liverpool and Leeds United
10. Loftus Road

QUIZ No. 24 ARSENAL – SEASON 2004/05

1. Dennis Bergkamp
2. Paul Scholes
3. Middlesbrough and Nottingham Forest
4. Blackburn Rovers
5. Arturo Lupoli
6. Manchester
7. Manchester United and Pizzagate
8. Thierry Henry
9. Everton
10. Sol Campbell and Robin Van Persie

QUIZ No. 25 ARSENAL – SEASON 2005/06

1. West Ham United
2. Middlesbrough and Alexandr Hleb
3. David Bentley
4. Robert Pires

5. Kanu
6. The first 70,000-plus Premier League crowd
7. Emmanuel Adebayor
8. It was his 100th Highbury goal
9. Sunderland
10. Spurs

QUIZ No. 26 ARSENAL – SEASON 2006/07

1. Liverpool
2. West Ham United and Bobby Zamora
3. Cesc Fabregas
4. Gilberto Silva
5. Bolton Wanderers
6. Tomas Rosicky
7. Peter Crouch
8. Kolo Toure and Emmanuel Adebayor
9. Julio Baptista
10. Blackburn Rovers

QUIZ No. 27 ARSENAL – SEASON 2007/08

1. Gael Glichy
2. Derby County and Adebayor
3. Middlesbrough
4. William Gallas
5. Newcastle United
6. Bolton Wanderers
7. Mikel Arteta
8. Fulham
9. Eduardo
10. Theo Walcott

QUIZ No. 28 ARSENAL – SEASON 2008/09

1. Carlos Vela
2. Spurs
3. Andrey Arshavin
4. Burnley
5. Blackburn Rovers
6. 0-0
7. Cardiff City
8. Jeremie Aliadiere
9. Brian Kidd
10. Chelsea

QUIZ No. 29 ARSENAL – SEASON 2009/10

1. 6-1
2. Thomas Vermaelen
3. Cesc Fabregas
4. Stoke City
5. Manchester City
6. Blackburn Rovers, Bolton Wanderers and Burnley
7. Six
8. Two own goals
9. Arsenal won 3-1
10. Wigan Athletic. The players allegedly came home by train after a disgusted Arsene Wenger dropped them at the station

QUIZ No. 30 ARSENAL – SEASON 2010/11

1. Ipswich Town
2. Newcastle United
3. Blackpool and Marouane Chamakh
4. Robin Van Persie
5. Jack Wilshere, Laurent Koscielny and Bacari Sagny
6. Leeds United and Huddersfield Town
7. Nicklas Bendtner
8. Aaron Ramsey
9. Jermaine Pennant
10. Andrey Arshavin

QUIZ No. 31 ARSENAL – SEASON 2011/12

1. 19
2. Alan Shearer and Thierry Henry
3. Manchester United got eight and Blackburn Rovers conceded seven
4. Manchester City and Sunderland
5. Aston Villa
6. Gervinho
7. 5-3
8. Thomas Vermaelen
9. 2003/04
10. Pat Rice

QUIZ No. 32 ARSENAL – SEASON 2012/13

1. Lukas Podolski
2. Blackburn Rovers and Bradford City
3. Theo Walcott
4. Jack Wilshere
5. Andre Santos
6. Emmanuel Adebayor and Per Mertesacker
7. Mikel Arteta
8. Santi Cazorla
9. Nacho Monreal
10. West Brom

QUIZ No. 33 ARSENAL – SEASON 2013/14

1. Aston Villa
2. Alex Oxlade-Chamberlain and Mikel Arteta
3. Sunderland and Paulo Di Canio
4. Serge Gnabry
5. Norwich City
6. Aaron Ramsey – the goals were against his former club Cardiff City
7. They lost 6-3
8. Carl Jenkinson
9. Per Mertesacker
10. Everton (against Sheffield Wednesday in 1966)

QUIZ No. 34 ARSENAL – SEASON 2014/15

1. 19th final – 12th win
2. Alexis Sanchez
3. Danny Welbeck
4. Santi Cazorla
5. Mathieu Debuchy
6. Aston Villa
7. Reading
8. Manchester City
9. Brighton & Hove Albion
10. George Robledo

QUIZ No. 35 ARSENAL – SEASON 2015/16

1. 2004/05
2. 5-2
3. Arsenal beat Aston Villa and Newcastle United beat Spurs
4. Hull City
5. Sunderland
6. Olivier Giroud
7. Alex Iwobi

8. Watford knocked them out and Blackburn Rovers kept their record intact
9. Andy Carroll
10. Alexis Sanchez and Danny Welbeck

QUIZ No. 36 ARSENAL - SEASON 2016/17

1. 1997/98 and 1994/95
2. Southampton
3. Alexis Sanchez
4. Southampton, Stoke City, Sunderland and Swansea City
5. Olivier Giroud against Crystal Palace
6. Bournemouth
7. Sutton United and Lincoln City
8. Per Mertesacker
9. Burnley
10. Everton

QUIZ No. 37 ARSENAL - SEASON 2017/18

1. Manchester City and Manchester United
2. Granit Xhaka
3. Danny Welbeck
4. Nottingham Forest
5. Leicester City
6. David Luiz
7. Aaron Ramsey and Ronald Koeman
8. Gareth Barry
9. Stoke City
10. A new Premier League attendance record of 83,222

QUIZ No. 38 ARSENAL - SEASON 2018/19

1. Crystal Palace
2. Blackpool
3. Joe Willock and Danny Welbeck
4. Fulham and Liverpool
5. Ainsley Maitland-Niles
6. Lucas Torreira
7. 32 years
8. Southampton
9. Pierre-Emerick Aubameyang
10. Sadio Mane and Mohamed Salah

QUIZ No. 39 ARSENAL - SEASON 2019/20

1. 100
2. Nacho Monreal and Nicolas Pepe
3. Gabriel Martinelli
4. David Luiz
5. Southampton and Norwich
6. Pierre-Emerick Aubameyang
7. Reiss Nelson
8. Leeds United, Sheffield United, Bournemouth and Portsmouth
9. West Ham United and Manchester City
10. Cedric Soares

QUIZ No. 40 ARSENAL V SPURS - LEAGUE 1900-99

1. The Manor Ground
2. Ted Drake
3. Dave Bowen
4. Ray Kennedy
5. No goals were scored
6. Paul Dickov
7. Liam Brady
8. 4-4
9. Tommy Lawton
10. Jackie Chalmers

QUIZ No. 41 ARSENAL V SPURS - CUP COMPETITIONS 1900-99

1. 1949
2. John Radford
3. Osvaldo Ardiles
4. Pat Jennings
5. Clive Allen
6. Viv Anderson and Ian Allinson
7. David Rocastle
8. Alan Smith
9. Tony Adams
10. 'The Donkey won the derby'

QUIZ No. 42 ARSENAL V SPURS - LEAGUE 2000-20

1. One
2. Five in 2004/05
3. Emmanuel Adebayor
4. 1-1
5. Patrick Vieira
6. 5-2
7. The Emirates in 2008/09
8. Olivier Giroud and Tomas Rosicky

9.   Van Persie and Van de Vaart
10. Kieran Gibbs

QUIZ No. 43 ARSENAL V SPURS - CUP COMPETITIONS 2000-20

1.   Patrick Vieira and Robert Pires
2.   Julio Baptista
3.   Adebayor and Arshavin
4.   Theo Walcott
5.   Nicklas Bendtner
6.   Samir Nasri
7.   Mathieu Flamini
8.   Calum Chambers
9.   2-0
10. Chelsea

QUIZ No. 44 ARSENE'S ASIDES

1.   Robin Van Persie
2.   Jose Mourinho
3.   Barcelona
4.   Alex Ferguson
5.   Jose Antonio Reyes
6.   Sausage
7.   Cesc Fabregas
8.   To stage the World Cup every two years
9.   Chelsea – it was his 1,000th game in charge of Arsenal
10. Wayne Rooney

QUIZ No. 45 ASSORTED GUNNERS - PART 1

1.   Rob Holding
2.   Marc Overmars
3.   Bernard Joy
4.   Luis Boa-Morte
5.   David Hannah
6.   Jimmy Carter
7.   Peter Goring
8.   Tony Adams
9.   Billy McCullough – the scout in the popular TV cowboy series *Wagon Train* was called Flint McCullough
10. George Armstrong

QUIZ No. 46 ASSORTED GUNNERS - PART 2

1.   David Seaman and Paul Mariner
2.   Danny Clapton
3.   Freddie Cox
4.   Terry Mancini
5.   Bob Wilson and Ray Kennedy
6.   Vic and Perry Groves
7.   Charles Buchan
8.   Vince
9.   David Jack
10. Gus Caesar

QUIZ No. 47 BIRTHPLACES

1.   Bolton
2.   Pamplona
3.   Nottingham
4.   Aaron Ramsey
5.   Rotterdam
6.   Bob Wilson and John Lukic
7.   Ian Ure
8.   Hollins – Guildford, Keown – Oxford, Oxlade-Chamberlain – Portsmouth, Walcott – Newbury
9.   Stoke Newington
10. Tony Adams

QUIZ No. 48 CHRISTMAS CRACKERS

1.   Port Vale
2.   Spurs
3.   5-0
4.   Leicester City
5.   Alan Ball
6.   Lincoln City
7.   Bolton Wanderers
8.   Nine
9.   Sunderland
10. Three – 25, 26 and 27 December

QUIZ No. 49 CRICKETING CONNECTIONS

1.   Alan Ball
2.   John Leather
3.   Jim Standen
4.   Bill Spittle
5.   Denis Compton
6.   Arthur Milton
7.   Steve Gatting
8.   Harry White
9.   Kieran Gibbs
10. Sammy Nelson

QUIZ No. 50 CUP CAPTAINS

1.   Tom Parker
2.   Alex James

3. Joe Mercer
4. Frank McLintock
5. Pat Rice
6. Kenny Sansom
7. Tony Adams
8. David Seaman
9. Patrick Vieira
10. Per Mertesacker

QUIZ No. 51 THE EMIRATES - PART 1

1. A rubbish processing plant
2. Ashburton Grove
3. The Arsenal Stadium
4. Aston Villa and Olof Mellberg
5. They all finished 1-1 after 90 minutes
6. 390 million
7. Gilberto Silva
8. Tony Adams, Thierry Henry and Dennis Bergkamp
9. Bolton Wanderers
10. Ascot

QUIZ No. 52 THE EMIRATES - PART 2

1. Abou Diaby
2. The Duke of Edinburgh stood in for the Queen
3. Spurs
4. Brazil
5. Bruce Springsteen
6. 2028
7. 60,704
8. Manchester United and Spurs
9. 26,000
10. Manchester United

QUIZ No. 53 FA CUP FINALS - CLUBS

1. Chelsea
2. Liverpool
3. Newcastle United
4. Cardiff City, Ipswich Town and Leeds United
5. West Ham United
6. Huddersfield Town, Sheffield United and Sheffield Wednesday
7. Sheffield Wednesday
8. Aston Villa

9. Newcastle United, Liverpool, Manchester United and Hull City
10. Sheffield United

QUIZ No. 54 FA CUP FINALS - PLAYERS

1. Alexis Sanchez, Freddie Ljungberg and Aaron Ramsey
2. John Lewis
3. Wally Barnes
4. Brian Talbot and Paul Mariner
5. James Chester of Hull City
6. Alan Ball
7. Steve Heighway and David Hirst
8. George Kennedy
9. Andy Linighan, Laurent Koscielny and Per Mertesacker
10. Ray Parlour and Robert Pires

QUIZ No. 55 FANS

1. Melvyn Bragg
2. Ian Poulter
3. An asteroid
4. Tony McCoy and Frankie Dettori
5. Dido
6. Fidel Castro
7. Geoffrey Palmer
8. Tom Watt
9. Spike Lee and Jay-Z
10. Dave Gilmour and Roger Waters

QUIZ No. 56 FOOTBALLER OF THE YEAR

1. Joe Mercer
2. Liam Brady
3. Charlie Nicholas and John Hartson
4. Frank McLintock
5. Dennis Bergkamp
6. Tony Adams and Paul Merson
7. Robert Pires
8. Thierry Henry
9. Robin Van Persie
10. Cesc Fabregas and Jack Wilshere

QUIZ No. 57 GOALKEEPERS - PART 1

1. David Ospina
2. Jens Lehmann
3. Richard Wright
4. Jimmy Rimmer
5. Jack Kelsey

6. George Swindin
7. Wilson – Alex in 1936 and Bob in 1971
8. Frank Moss
9. Dan Lewis
10. Celta Vigo

QUIZ No. 58 GOALKEEPERS – PART 2

1. Geoff Barnett
2. Tony Burns
3. Petr Cech
4. Bayer Leverkusen
5. QPR
6. Damien Martinez
7. Wojciech Szczesny
8. Pat Jennings and David Seaman
9. Lukasz Fabianski
10. Alex Manninger

QUIZ No. 59 GREENER GRASS

1. Anders Limpar
2. Michael Thomas
3. Sol Campbell, Nwankwo Kanu and Lassana Diarra
4. David Herd and Frank Stapleton
5. Geoff Strong
6. Patrick Vieira
7. Nicolas Anelka and Ashley Cole
8. Kolo Toure, Gael Clichy and Samir Nasri
9. Emmanuel Adebayor
10. Olivier Giroud and Cesc Fabregas

QUIZ No. 60 HAT-TRICKS

1. Marc Overmars
2. Sylvain Wiltord
3. Kevin Campbell
4. Ray Parlour
5. Carlos Vela
6. Brian Talbot
7. Joe Baker and Geoff Strong
8. Olivier Giroud
9. Mesut Ozil
10. Lucas Perez

QUIZ No. 61 HIGHBURY

1. The Archbishop of Canterbury
2. Leicester Fosse
3. Charles Buchan
4. Seven

5. Gillespie Road
6. Ted Drake
7. Tommy Lawton
8. Laurie Scott
9. Thierry Henry
10. Wigan Athletic again

QUIZ No. 62 HIGHBURY HEROES – No.1 – TONY ADAMS

1. He was born in 1966 and won 66 England caps
2. He is the only man to captain a club to the league title in three different decades, and the only man to play for England in a tournament over three different decades
3. Sunderland
4. Anfield
5. Celtic and Lee Dixon
6. Yugoslavia
7. It was the last England goal at the 'old' Wembley
8. They play at Adams Park
9. Joe Jordan
10. Less – he scored 48 goals

QUIZ No. 63 HIGHBURY HEROES – No. 2 – DENNIS BERGKAMP

1. Denis Law
2. Bruce Rioch and Inter Milan
3. Southampton and Hartlepool United
4. Leicester City
5. Oxford United
6. Paul Bracewell
7. Sol Campbell
8. West Bromwich Albion
9. Ajax
10. One of Wagner's operas was 'The Flying Dutchman'. After a scare aboard a plane Dennis never flew again and became the 'non-flying' Dutchman

QUIZ No. 64 HIGHBURY HEROES – No. 3 – HERBERT CHAPMAN

1. Northampton Town
2. Spurs
3. Leeds City
4. Huddersfield Town

5. Alex James and Cliff Bastin
6. 66
7. Three
8. 1934
9. Jimmy Brain and Jack Lambert
10. Jacob Epstein

QUIZ No. 65 HIGHBURY HEROES – No. 4 – TED DRAKE

1. Southampton
2. George Allison
3. Wolves
4. 42
5. Aston Villa
6. Stamford Bridge
7. Burnden Park
8. Reading
9. Chelsea
10. Joe Mercer and George Graham

QUIZ No. 66 HIGHBURY HEROES – No. 5 – GEORGE GRAHAM

1. Aston Villa
2. Two
3. As a player it was the only ground he scored twice on for Scotland. As a manager he was knocked out of the FA Cup there with Arsenal in January 1992
4. Chelsea and Crystal Palace
5. Charlie George scored the first goal
6. Millwall
7. Don Howe
8. Leeds United
9. Joe Hulme and Terry Neill
10. 'Man in a raincoat's blue and white army'

QUIZ No. 67 HIGHBURY HEROES – No. 6 – THIERRY HENRY

1. Juventus
2. Monaco
3. 83
4. The FA Cup
5. New York Red Bulls and Montreal Impact
6. Sergio Aguero
7. Leeds United and Sunderland
8. Belgium
9. William Gallas
10. Brendan Rodgers being sacked by Liverpool

QUIZ No. 68 HIGHBURY HEROES No. 7 – FRANK MCLINTOCK

1. Leicester City
2. Two for each club
3. Stoke City
4. Norway
5. Spain
6. Gillingham
7. Carlisle United and Cologne
8. West Bromwich Albion
9. QPR
10. Yes - 401

QUIZ No. 69 HIGHBURY HEROES – No. 8 – JOE MERCER

1. Everton
2. £7,000
3. Bolton Wanderers
4. Blackpool and Preston North End
5. He is the only man to win a league title with three different clubs, two as a player and one as a manager
6. England
7. Liverpool
8. The League Cup
9. Horseracing – Joe Mercer was a classic-winning flat jockey
10. It was his birthday

QUIZ No. 70 HIGHBURY HEROES – No. 9 – DAVID SEAMAN

1. Leeds United and Peterborough United
2. True – he played in 69
3. Wimbledon
4. Sheffield United and Paul Peschisolido
5. Saudi Arabia
6. Brian Marwood, Michael Thomas and Alan Smith
7. Birmingham City and Manchester City
8. Joe Hart
9. Michael Owen
10. 560

QUIZ No. 71 HIGHBURY HEROES – No. 10 – PATRICK VIEIRA

1. Cannes
2. Milan
3. More – 107

4. The League Cup
5. Sheffield Wednesday and Derby County
6. True
7. Sunderland and Liverpool
8. The winning penalty in the shoot-out to decide the 2005 FA Cup Final against Manchester United
9. Juventus
10. New York City and Nice

QUIZ No. 72 HIGHBURY HEROES – No. 11 – ARSENE WENGER

1. Blackburn Rovers and Huddersfield Town
2. Nancy and Nagoya Grampas 8
3. Glenn Hoddle and Jurgen Klinsmann
4. The FA Cup – seven times
5. Nicolas Anelka
6. Inspector Clouseau
7. George Allison
8. Tony Adams
9. Ian Wright and Pierre-Emerick Aubameyang
10. Burnley

QUIZ No. 73 HIGHBURY HEROES – No. 12 – IAN WRIGHT

1. Crystal Palace
2. Frank Stapleton
3. The League Cup
4. Burnley
5. Cameroon
6. Poland
7. Bolton Wanderers and Cliff Bastin
8. Everton
9. Celtic and Nottingham Forest
10. Southampton

QUIZ No. 74 THE 100 CLUB

1. Jimmy Brain
2. Reg Lewis and Thierry Henry
3. Paul Merson
4. Joe Baker
5. David Herd, George Graham, Frank Stapleton and Robin Van Persie all went to Manchester United
6. Dennis Bergkamp
7. Frank Stapleton and Alan Sunderland
8. Thierry Henry, Ian Wright, Cliff Bastin and John Radford
9. Cliff Bastin
10. Ted Drake

QUIZ No. 75 INTERNATIONALS – ENGLAND (POST-WAR)

1. Franny Jeffers and Carl Jenkinson
2. Leslie Compton
3. Jeff Blockley and Steve Bould
4. Ashley Cole
5. Joe Baker and Tony Woodcock
6. Tony Adams, Ray Parlour and David Seaman
7. David Platt
8. Smith – Lionel and Alan, and Wright – Ian and Richard
9. Alan Ball and Martin Keown
10. Dixon got 22 and Winterburn got two

QUIZ No. 76 INTERNATIONALS – SCOTLAND AND WALES (POST-WAR)

1. Ray Daniel
2. Tommy Docherty
3. Aaron Ramsey
4. Jimmy Logie
5. Dave Bowen
6. Ian Ure
7. Mel Charles
8. Alex Forbes
9. John Hartson
10. Jackie Henderson

QUIZ No. 77 INTERNATIONALS – NORTHERN IRELAND AND THE REPUBLIC (POST-WAR)

1. Steve Morrow
2. West Ham United
3. Brighton & Hove Albion
4. Manchester City and Sunderland
5. Pat Rice
6. Joe Haverty
7. Terry Neill
8. David O'Leary
9. John McClelland
10. Ajax and Le Havre

QUIZ No. 78 INTERNATIONALS – OVERSEAS – PART 1

1. Switzerland
2. Ivory Coast
3. Latvia
4. Belgium
5. Colombia
6. Armenia
7. Egypt
8. Greece
9. Uruguay
10. Togo

QUIZ No. 79 INTERNATIONALS – OVERSEAS – PART 2

1. Cameroon
2. Austria
3. Russia
4. Denmark
5. Ghana
6. Spain
7. Czech Republic
8. France
9. Chile
10. Nigeria

QUIZ No. 80 LEAGUE CUP FINALS

1. Bobby Gould
2. Charlie Nicholas
3. Perry Groves and Martin Hayes
4. Paul Merson and Steve Morrow
5. Players' names appeared on the backs of their shirts for the first time in a Wembley final
6. Theo Walcott
7. Robin Van Persie
8. Don Rogers, Brian Stein and Didier Drogba
9. Swindon Town, Luton Town and Manchester City
10. Nigel Winterburn

QUIZ No. 81 MAD MATCHES

1. 5-5
2. 6-4 to Sheffield United
3. 17 – Arsenal won 6-3 and drew 4-4
4. Leicester City
5. Manchester City and Newcastle United
6. 5-4
7. Notts County
8. Aston Villa
9. 5-5
10. 7-4

QUIZ No. 82 MANAGERS

1. George Graham
2. Phil Kelso
3. Herbert Chapman
4. Bertie Mee
5. Bruce Rioch and Mikel Arteta
6. George Swindin
7. Billy Wright
8. Don Howe, Brian Talbot and Bobby Gould
9. Tom Whittaker
10. More – by seven to six

QUIZ No. 83 MULTIPLE CHOICE

1. Leeds United
2. Sheffield Wednesday
3. Liverpool
4. Lee Dixon
5. Newcastle United
6. Everton
7. George Swindin
8. Preston North End
9. Paris
10. Sheffield

QUIZ No. 84 OPENING DAYS

1. Seven
2. It was the first *Match of the Day* on television
3. John Radford
4. Norwich City
5. Blackpool and Brighton & Hove Albion
6. Goodison Park
7. Leyton Orient
8. Bury
9. Ted Drake
10. Wimbledon

QUIZ No. 85 OUTGUNNED BY PEASHOOTERS – (GIANT KILLING)

1. Walsall
2. Norwich City
3. Bedford Town
4. Northampton Town
5. Peterborough United
6. Tranmere Rovers

7. York City
8. Keith Houchen
9. Wrexham
10. Bradford City

QUIZ No. 86 PENALTIES

1. Fergus Hunt
2. Port Vale and West Ham United
3. Leicester City
4. Jimmy Sharp
5. Peter Storey
6. Reg Lewis and Leeds United
7. Thierry Henry, Robert Pires and Manchester City
8. Wally Barnes
9. Rotherham United, Sheffield United and Doncaster Rovers
10. Roberto Mancini and Attilio Lombardo

QUIZ No. 87 QUOTES

1. Brian Clough
2. Ruud Van Nistelrooy
3. Ian Wright
4. Alan Sugar
5. Dave Bassett
6. Nigel Worthington
7. Brian Marwood
8. Jose Antonio Reyes
9. Tony Adams
10. Jose Mourinho

QUIZ No. 88 RECKLESS REDS

1. Kolo Toure and Emmanuel Adebayor
2. Alan Ball
3. Martin Keown
4. Patrick Vieira
5. Ray Parlour
6. Jason Crowe
7. Paul Davis
8. Wojciech Szczesny
9. Jermaine Pennant
10. Jose Antonio Reyes

QUIZ No. 89 SHARPSHOOTERS

1. Jack Lambert
2. Alan Smith
3. Doug Lishman
4. Seven
5. Ian Wright, Tony Woodcock and Theo Walcott
6. Nicolas Anelka, Emmanuel

Adebayor and Pierre-Emerick Aubameyang
7. Brian Kidd and Ray Kennedy
8. Ted Drake
9. Cesc Fabregas
10. Four

QUIZ No. 90 TRANSFERS – 1946-59

1. Derek Tapscott
2. Leyton Orient
3. Southampton
4. Brentford
5. Bill Dodgin
6. Doug Lishman
7. Jim Fotheringham
8. David Herd
9. Tommy Docherty
10. Ronnie Rooke

QUIZ No. 91 TRANSFERS – 1960s

1. Dundee and Hibernian
2. George Eastham – Newcastle United and Stoke City
3. Birmingham City and Blackpool
4. Joe Baker
5. Eddie Clamp
6. John Barnwell
7. Jim Furnell
8. Dave Bacuzzi
9. Don Howe
10. Bobby Gould

QUIZ No. 92 TRANSFERS – 1970s

1. Wolves
2. Pat Howard
3. Willie Young and Steve Walford
4. Bob McNab
5. Southampton, Portsmouth and Hull City
6. Fulham and West Ham United
7. Stoke City and Seattle Sounders
8. Brian Kidd
9. QPR
10. Leicester City

QUIZ No. 93 TRANSFERS – 1980s

1. Stewart Robson
2. Oxford United
3. Lee Dixon and Steve Bould
4. Portsmouth
5. Steve Williams
6. Pat Rice and Kevin Richardson

7. Nigel Winterburn
8. Juventus
9. Crystal Palace
10. Colchester United

QUIZ No. 94 TRANSFERS - 1990s

1. Luton Town
2. Manu Petit and Gilles Grimandi
3. Nottingham Forest
4. QPR
5. Nwankwo Kanu
6. Norwich City
7. West Ham United
8. John Lukic and David Rocastle
9. Middlesbrough
10. Bristol City

QUIZ No. 95 TRANSFERS - 2000s

1. William Gallas
2. Servette
3. Armand Traore
4. Borussia Dortmund
5. Feyenoord and Ajax
6. Cannes and Bordeaux
7. Auxerre
8. Marseilles
9. Giovanni Van Bronckhorst
10. Atalanta

QUIZ No. 96 TRANSFERS - 2010s

1. Barcelona
2. Southampton
3. Malaga
4. Lorient
5. AC Milan
6. Santi Cazorla
7. Olivier Giroud and Alexandre Lacazette
8. Charlton Athletic
9. Sokratis
10. Shkodran Mustafi

QUIZ No. 97 TRUE OR FALSE - PART 1

1. True
2. True
3. False – Fulham lost to Atletico Madrid in the first one
4. True
5. True
6. False – it is four
7. False – it happened five times
8. True

9. True
10. False – it's 21 – 20 to Quinn

QUIZ No. 98 TRUE OR FALSE - PART 2

1. True
2. False – Pat Jennings played in the 1970s and 1980s
3. True
4. True
5. False – the score is 7-7
6. True
7. False – it should be six, Leicester City are missing
8. False – they won 22 in 1968/69
9. False – they finished bottom of Division One in 1912/13
10. True

QUIZ No. 99 VENUES

1. The Victoria Ground, Stoke
2. Stamford Bridge
3. Goodison Park
4. Villa Park
5. Old Trafford
6. The Millennium Stadium, Cardiff
7. Highfield Road, Coventry
8. The 'new' Wembley
9. Birmingham
10. Leeds Road, Huddersfield

QUIZ No. 100 WHICH, WHAT, HOW, WHO AND WHY?

1. Aston Villa
2. They are all Arsenal players, making six, 110 and 280 appearances respectively
3. Shaw – seven times
4. John Hartson
5. Spurs
6. Leeds United
7. It was the League South Cup of 1942/43 during World War Two
8. Lambert and Butler
9. Blackpool
10. Brentford

INTRODUCTION QUESTION

The Milk Marketing Board, Coca-Cola, Worthington, Carling And Carabao.